STD

OVERSIZE

3.3.80

THE ARCO BOOK OF
HOME PLANS

JEROLD L. AXELROD
Architect

ARCO PUBLISHING, INC.
NEW YORK

Published by Arco Publishing, Inc.
219 Park Avenue South, New York, N.Y. 10003

Library of Congress Cataloging in Publication Data

Axelrod, Jerold L
   The Arco book of home plans.

   1. Architecture, Domestic—Designs and plans.
I. Title.
NA7115.A93 1979 728.3   79-14620
ISBN 0-668-04728-3 (Library Edition)
ISBN 0-668-04732-1 (Paper Edition)

Printed in the United States of America

Information regarding the ordering of stock plans for the homes in this book may be obtained by writing the author, Jerold L. Axelrod, Architect, 275 Broadhollow Road., Melville, N.Y. 11746

Foreword

Many decisions must be made by a family considering the construction of a new home, but the most critical is the selection of the design itself. This pictorial guide is one of the most complete volumes of home plans ever published. In addition to the many fine homes presented, you will also find within these covers a wealth of invaluable information to help you to choose the right home. This book will provide you with the basic tools needed to make your dream into a reality.

The Arco Book of Home Plans is not a "how to build a home" book; there are many such volumes available to you. It is, however, the perfect primer to get you started, and help you to select the proper home to fit your needs and your lifestyle. Included are articles on using stock plans, making changes in a stock design, choosing the right home and site, or making the most of the site you own. There is also an extensive section on energy conservation techniques, including solar heating, and some excellent suggestions for commonly overlooked ways to save money, whether you are going to hire a contractor or do it yourself.

Most important, however, are the home plans themselves. This book includes seventy two individual homes, each an outstanding and distinctive design—no dated, repetitive, look-alikes here. Each home was carefully chosen as the best of the many plans in our files having the same size and style. Therefore, this book presents for your viewing an enormous variety of home designs; homes of all sizes and the widest selection of styles, suited for different budgets, tastes, even lot conditions. There should be a home here to satisfy you, and construction blueprints are available on all of the homes.

Understanding the Material Lists

One of the bonuses of this book is the inclusion of an abbreviated material list for each home design shown. The typical page for each home includes an artist's rendering of the exterior view, floor plan or plans, a short written description of the design, data on the size of the home, and a list of required quantities of the major construction elements. These statistics should be a valuable aid to evaluating the relative costs of each home design.

The size of the home is given in square footage of living area, which does not include garages or porches. It is measured as gross floor area including all walls (the recognized standard). The quantities in the material lists use the following abbreviations:

(s)	= slab–no basement	s.f.	= square feet
(b)	= basement	l.f.	= lineal feet
c.y.	= cubic yards	b.f.	= board foot measure
c.f.	= cubic feet	s.y.	= square yards

The quantities shown are summaries only (a detailed list is included with orders of construction blueprints from the author); however, these summaries should be useful in a number of ways. By taking the listing of a particular house you have in mind to your local materials supplier, you can get a rough approximation of the cost of the major construction materials required. Most lists give quantities for both slab construction (no basement) and for basement, so you can approximate the additional materials required for a basement.

Finally, by analyzing the quantities of one house against any other, you can get a relative idea of potential cost differences. This could afford you many hours of interesting comparisons.

Contents

About Stock Plans

Who Buys Stock Plans?

In most communities, professional architectural talent to design a custom home is not available. In those cities where such services are available, only a handful of potential homebuyers can afford the full scope of such services, which can run into thousands of dollars. Even among those who can afford such specialized services, there are many who find it easier to choose a "ready-made," pre-designed, pre-tested home rather than go through the process of having one designed especially for them. These people buy stock plans.

What Are Stock Plans?

Most stock plans are custom homes. Many were designed for special clients, others for the general public. All the homes in this book were personally designed by the author, a practicing architect, with the same concern for detail, design integrity, and a quality, functional floor plan as I would strive for in designing a custom home for an individual client. The working drawings, commonly referred to as blueprints, which are available for purchase together with the specifications and materials list, were also prepared under my direction with this same concern for quality.

Arranged for individually, such services could amount to several thousand dollars. Stock plans are made available at a mere fraction of their value by virtue of a large general publication. They are, for that reason, probably the biggest bargain you will encounter in the total expenditure for your home. As such, it is folly to select plans based solely on blueprint cost. Recognizing this, many people opt to purchase plans of several different homes, thus being able to thoroughly analyze each and have costs compared, before making the final decision to build.

The greatest achievement, then, of stock plans is that they provide the benefits of professional talent via a quality, well-designed home to many people who, otherwise, would not be able to take advantage of the opportunity.

Basic Limitations of Stock Plans

If stock plans are so great, why would anyone still want to pay to have a custom home designed personally for themselves? There are several compelling reasons. If someone has a very particular idea about how their home should look, or be planned, or if they have an unusual lot that requires a unique solution, it is possible that no existing stock plan will come close to satisfying the requirements. There is also the question of personal contact with the architect, and the resulting development of a home that becomes a very personal statement.

Stock plans have some major deficiencies. By definition, most stock plans must be capable of fitting general requirements rather than specific ones. They fit average lot conditions, and they exchange information from architect to purchaser in an impersonal manner.

Accepting these limitations, however, does not preclude good design. It does present a special challenge to the architect, to create a distinctive home, such as the ones in this book. It also requires a special care on the part of the purchaser of a stock plan to retain the integrity of the design throughout construction, particularly if changes are contemplated.

THIS IS A COVER HOUSE

THE MONTERREY

A modest, contemporary ranch that looks, lives and functions as comfortably as homes much larger in size. Upon entering, the reception foyer affords an immediate view of the living room with its cathedral ceiling, brick fireplace and wraparound corner windows. A spacious country kitchen includes a breakfast bar, a pantry and sliding glass doors to the rear porch—with a barbecue under the porch roof. The barbecue is backed-up to a second fireplace located in the charming kitchen. The master bedroom features a dressing area and walk-in closet, as well as a private full bath.

AREA DATA   Living Area   1,285 s.f.
            Opt. Basement   1,356 s.f.

FLOOR PLAN

58⁴

51⁰

MASTER BEDROOM 15⁸x12⁰
DRESS — WALK-IN CLOSET
BATH — BATH
BEDROOM 10⁰x11⁰
DEN / B.R.#3/ DIN. RM. 12⁴/10⁰x9⁰
FOYER
LIVING ROOM 19⁰x13⁰ CATHEDRAL CEIL'G
FIREPL
PORCH 14⁴x16⁴ BARBECUE
SLID. DR.
FIREPL
COUNTRY KITCHEN 14⁰x21⁰
PAN
BREAKFAST BAR
REF — S — DW
FURN
MUD ROOM
D W — S
STORAGE
2 CAR GARAGE 20⁰x20⁰
LINE OF ONE CAR GARAGE
PORCH

MATERIAL LIST

Concrete	(s)	64 c.y.	Windows (sliding)		9
	(b)	92 c.y.	(fixed)		2
Brick Veneer		200 s.f.	Doors (exterior)		3
Framing Lumber	(s)	9,367 b.f.	(ext. sliding)		2
	(b)	12,286 b.f.	(interior swing)		7
			(int. closet)		4
Wall Sheathing		1,370 s.f.	Texture 1-11		1,300 s.f.
Roof Sheathing		3,000 s.f.	Asphalt Shingles		3,000 s.f.
Sub Flooring		1,350 s.f.	½'' Gypsum Drywall		5,810 s.f.
3½'' Wall Insulation		1,260 s.f.	Ceramic Tile		209 s.f.
6'' Ceiling Insulation		1,440 s.f.	Vinyl Tile		295 s.f.
1'' x 24'' Slab Insulation		150 l.f.	Carpet		63 s.y.

7

THE ADMIRAL

A charming, colonial style (center hall) two story home, designed for luxurious living. The living and dining rooms, flanking the entrance foyer, include bayed front windows with built-in window seats. The family room features a sunken conversation area with a fireplace, log bin and wet bar. The kitchen provides a very large work area, plus a separate bay windowed dinette. A large laundry-sewing room provides access to the side entry two car garage and the yard. There are four bedrooms and a compartmented hall bath on the second floor. The master bedroom features a vaulted ceiling, two walk-in closets and a private full bath.

AREA DATA

First Floor	1,471 s.f.
Second Floor	1,279 s.f.
Basement	1,008 s.f.
Overall Dimensions	60' x 41'

MATERIAL LIST

Concrete	73 c.y.	Doors (exterior)	3
Brick Veneer	130 s.f.	(interior swing)	16
Framing Lumber	14,912 b.f.	(int. closet)	3
Wall Sheathing	3,100 s.f.	Wood Shakes	2,860 s.f.
Roof Sheathing	2,510 s.f.	Asphalt Shingles	2,510 s.f.
Sub Flooring	2,230 s.f.	½'' Gypsum Drywall	8,600 s.f.
3½'' Wall Insulation	2,380 s.f.	Ceramic Tile	250 s.f.
6'' Ceiling Insulation	1,640 s.f.	Vinyl Tile	362 s.f.
1'' x 24'' Slab Insulation	54 l.f.	Oak Flooring	1,860 s.f.
Windows (double hung)	20	Carpet	157 s.y.
(fixed)	1		
(basement)	3		

A large, well zoned, contemporary ranch, designed to capture a rear view. All major rooms, including the master bedroom, face onto a wraparound rear deck, with access from the eat-in kitchen, living room and dining room. An open feeling predominates in the entertaining area, highlighted by a step down conversation pit and fireplace. The rear of the fireplace serves as a focal point in the foyer. Privacy is assured to the sloped ceiling master bedroom. Although modest in frontage requirements, the facade is not lacking in curb appeal; a walled, atrium-style entrance court flanked by two contrasting front gable roofs create a striking exterior.

MATERIAL LIST

Concrete	(s)	75 c.y.
	(b)	105 c.y.
Brick Veneer		100 s.f.
Flitch Plates		1
Framing Lumber	(s)	8,086 b.f.
	(b)	12,379 b.f.
Wall Sheathing		1,780 s.f.
Roof Sheathing		3,380 s.f.
Sub Flooring		2,040 s.f.
3½″ Wall Insulation		1,540 s.f.
6″ Ceiling Insulation		2,120 s.f.
1″ x 24″ Slab Insulation		200 l.f.
Windows (sliding)		11
(fixed)		7
Doors (exterior)		2
(ext. sliding)		4
(interior swing)		11
(int. closet)		5
Texture 1-11 Siding		1,700 s.f.
Asphalt Shingles		3,380 s.f.
½″ Gypsum Drywall		6,275 s.f.
Ceramic Tile		294 s.f.
Vinyl Tile		214 s.f.
Oak Flooring		1,370 s.f.
Carpet		18 s.y.

THE BERKELEY

AREA DATA	Living Area	2,678 s.f.
	Opt. Basement	2,678 s.f.

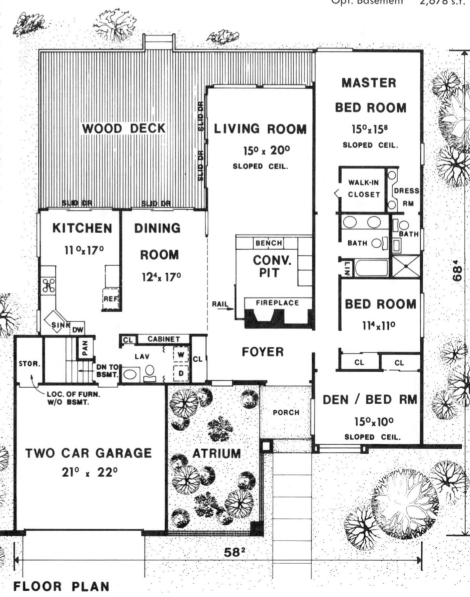

FLOOR PLAN

THE SYCAMORE

A contemporary "Cape Cod" with exterior appeal deriving from a combination of stone veneer, rustic board and batten, and barn sidings. Inside, a soaring cathedral ceiling joins the foyer and living room. The U-shape kitchen and adjoining family room feature a desk, snack bar and sliding glass doors to the patio. The dining room with its circular style bay window creates a distinctive space. The master bedroom includes dual walk-in closets, a private full shower-bath and a vaulted ceiling. The second floor provides for three additional bedrooms and a third full bath but, since there are no bearing partitions on this floor, it can be laid out with great freedom to suit your needs.

AREA DATA	First Floor	1,407 s.f.
	Second Floor	612 s.f.
	Opt. Basement	1,277 s.f.

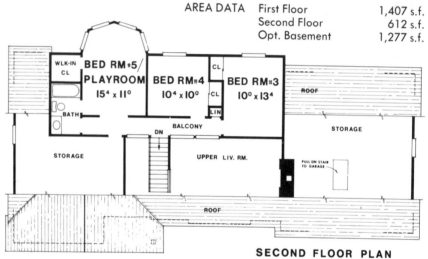

SECOND FLOOR PLAN

MATERIAL LIST

Concrete	(s)	55 c.y.
	(b)	86 c.y.
Stone Veneer		182 s.f.
Framing Lumber	(s)	8,762 b.f.
	(b)	13,249 b.f.
Wall Sheathing		2,180 s.f.
Roof Sheathing		2,420 s.f.
Sub Flooring		2,140 s.f.
3½'' Wall Insulation		1,880 s.f.
6'' Ceiling Insulation		1,510 s.f.
1'' x 24'' Slab Insulation		80 l.f.
Windows (sliding)		23
Doors (exterior)		3
(ext. sliding)		1
(interior swing)		18
(int. closet)		6
Rough Sawn Plywd. (3/8'')		1,920 s.f.
Asphalt Shingles		2,500 s.f.
½'' Gypsum Drywall		6,760 s.f.
Ceramic Tile		300 s.f.
Vinyl Tile		350 s.f.
Oak Flooring		156 s.f.
Carpet		155 s.y.

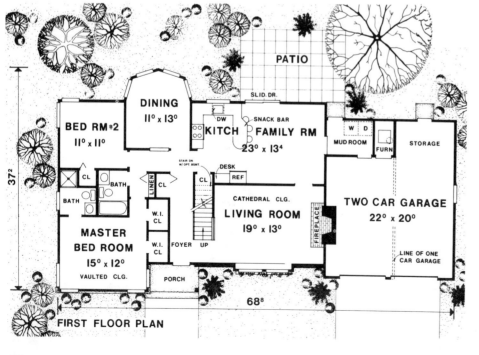

FIRST FLOOR PLAN

THE CARLISLE

The elegant brick front of this handsome, Georgian style, two story colonial home is suggestive of the quality of the interior. To the left of the gracious central foyer are the living and dining rooms. Opposite the living room is the family room; fireplaces are available in both areas. A spacious eat-in kitchen with a bayed breakfast area is centrally located for ease of circulation. A mud room, powder room and two car garage round out the first floor. The second floor features four bedrooms and two full baths. The master suite includes a dressing room, two closets, an optional fireplace and a modest balcony. Blueprints include slab or basement versions.

AREA DATA	First Floor	1,150 s.f.
	Second Floor	1,131 s.f.
	Opt. Basement	771 s.f.

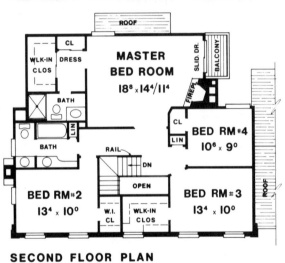

SECOND FLOOR PLAN

MATERIAL LIST

Concrete	(s)	42 c.y.
	(b)	60 c.y.
Brick Veneer		452 s.f.
Flitch Plates		2
Framing Lumber	(s)	9,431 b.f.
	(b)	11,277 b.f.
Wall Sheathing		2,270 s.f.
Roof Sheathing		1,810 s.f.
Sub Flooring		1,091 s.f.
3½'' Wall Insulation		1,940 s.f.
6'' Ceiling Insulation		1,160 s.f.
1'' x 24'' Slab Insulation		127 l.f.
Windows (single hung)		19
(fixed)		2
Doors (exterior)		2
(ext. sliding)		2
(interior swing)		16
(int. closet)		4
Wood Shingles		1,920 s.f.
Asphalt Shingles		1,810 s.f.
½'' Gypsum Drywall		8,452 s.f.
Ceramic Tile		255 s.f.
Vinyl Tile		251 s.f.
Carpet		172 s.y.

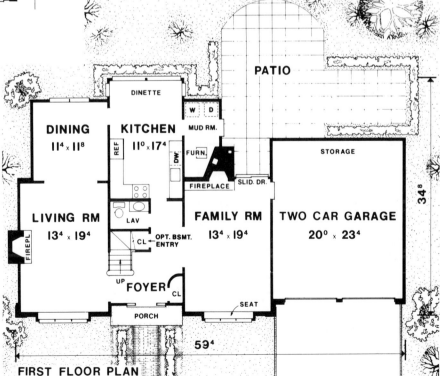

FIRST FLOOR PLAN

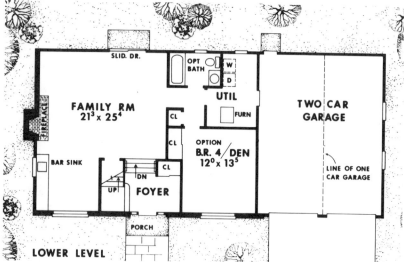

LOWER LEVEL

- SLID. DR.
- OPT BATH
- W / D
- UTIL
- FAMILY RM 21³ x 25⁴
- FIREPLACE
- TWO CAR GARAGE
- CL
- CL
- FURN
- CL
- OPTION B.R. 4/DEN 12⁰ x 13⁵
- BAR SINK
- DN
- UP
- FOYER
- LINE OF ONE CAR GARAGE
- PORCH

THE GREENBRIAR

This unusual hi-ranch (bi-level or split-foyer) home is designed for spacious family living, along with economy by building up. A large central foyer with a closet and wide stairs up *and* down make for an unusually distinctive entrance. The upper living area consists of a spacious living room and a dining room with a bow window and sliding glass door to the outdoor deck. The corner kitchen is large enough to accommodate a full breakfast area. The upper level also contains three bedrooms, including the master bedroom with a huge closet and a private bath. The lower level includes a large family room with a wet bar and fireplace, an optional fourth bedroom, a mud room and two car garage.

AREA DATA

Upper Level	1,304 s.f.
Lower Level	600 s.f.
Opt. 4th Bedroom/Bath	366 s.f.
Overall Dimensions	48' x 28'

MATERIAL LIST

Concrete	40 c.y.
Brick Veneer	320 s.f.
Flitch Plate	1
Framing Lumber	9,182 b.f.
Wall Sheathing	2,040 s.f.
Roof Sheathing	1,590 s.f.
Sub Flooring	1,300 s.f.
3½" Wall Insulation	1,940 s.f.
6" Ceiling Insulation	1,300 s.f.
1" x 24" Slab Insulation	94 l.f.
Windows (sliding)	14
(bow window)	1
Doors (exterior)	2
(ext. sliding)	2
(interior swing)	10
(int. closet)	5
Exterior Siding	1,720 s.f.
Asphalt Shingles	1,600 s.f.
½" Gypsum Drywall	7,350 s.f.
Ceramic Tile	322 s.f.
Vinyl Tile	802 s.f.
Oak Flooring	915 s.f.

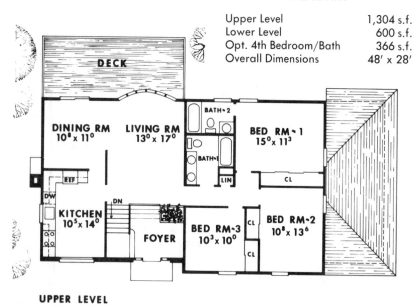

UPPER LEVEL

- DECK
- DINING RM 10⁸ x 11⁰
- LIVING RM 13⁰ x 17⁰
- BATH-2
- BED RM-1 15⁰ x 11³
- BATH-1
- REF
- LIN
- CL
- DW
- KITCHEN 10⁵ x 14⁰
- DN
- FOYER
- BED RM-3 10³ x 10⁰
- BED RM-2 10⁸ x 13⁶
- CL
- CL

THE SEQUOIA

With its large expanses of glass, this contemporary vacation home can be situated on any site to provide maximum view. At under 1,300 sq. ft., it will be economical, yet it provides up to three bedrooms, two baths, ample kitchen and dining room, and a dramatic two story living area. A brick fireplace is the focal point of the living room, and the back of it also serves to enhance the kitchen. A raised entrance foyer provides for a distinct "place of entry" without detracting from the living room. Three separate decks on the rear of the house will provide many hours of relaxation and enjoyment.

AREA DATA   First Floor   878 s.f.
               Second Floor   416 s.f.
               Opt. Basement   878 s.f.

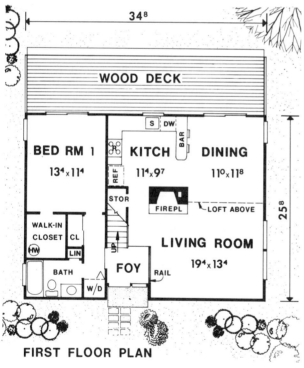

FIRST FLOOR PLAN

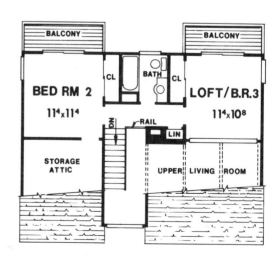

SECOND FLOOR PLAN

MATERIAL LIST

Concrete	(s)	27 c.y.	Doors (exterior)		1
	(b)	45 c.y.	(ext. sliding)		4
Framing Lumber	(s)	5,972 b.f.	(interior swing)		10
	(b)	7,525 b.f.	(int. closet)		4
Wall Sheathing		1,820 s.f.	Exterior Siding		1,820 s.f.
Roof Sheathing		1,040 s.f.	Asphalt Shingles		1,050 s.f.
Sub Flooring		500 s.f.	½'' Gypsum Drywall		4,900 s.f.
3½'' Wall Insulation		1,760 s.f.	Ceramic Tile		156 s.f.
6'' Ceiling Insulation		1,340 s.f.	Vinyl Tile		160 s.f.
1'' x 24'' Slab Insulation		125 l.f.	Oak Flooring		328 s.f.
Windows (sliding)		4	Carpet		63 s.y.
(fixed)		7			

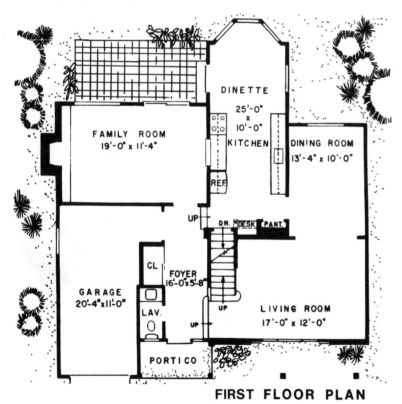

FIRST FLOOR PLAN

Within the plan:
DINETTE 25'-0" x 10'-0"
KITCHEN
FAMILY ROOM 19'-0" x 11'-4"
DINING ROOM 13'-4" x 10'-0"
REF
UP
DN. DESK PANT.
CL
FOYER 16'-0" x 5'-8"
GARAGE 20'-4" x 11'-0"
LAV.
UP
LIVING ROOM 17'-0" x 12'-0"
UP
PORTICO

THE LANCASTER

This charming four bedroom, two story, traditional style home has the distinction of providing a lovely, workable floor plan in a modest, practical size. It is entered via a covered front portico leading to a formal reception foyer. To the right is the living room with a colonial picture window; a formal dining room adjoins in an "L." The kitchen features a panoramic bay windowed dinette, a rear service door, a built-in desk and a pantry. The family room includes a fireplace with raised hearth, sliding glass doors and a beamed ceiling. The second floor provides four bedrooms and two full baths. A large basement is included.

AREA DATA		
	First Floor	1,045 s.f.
	Second Floor	860 s.f.
	Basement	646 s.f.
	Overall Dimensions	42' x 40'

SECOND FLOOR PLAN

Within the plan:
BED ROOM #2 11'-0" x 10'-0"
BED ROOM #3 11'-0" x 8'-6"
BED ROOM #4 13'-0" x 10'-6"
CL
CL LIN CL
HALL
CL CL
BATH #1
DN
#2
CL
BATH
DRESSING ROOM
MASTER BED ROOM 17'-0" x 12'-0"

MATERIAL LIST

Concrete	56 c.y.	Doors (exterior)	3
Brick Veneer	80 s.f.	(ext. sliding)	1
Framing Lumber	14,740 b.f.	(interior swing)	13
Wall Sheathing	2,380 s.f.	(int. closet)	3
Roof Sheathing	1,950 s.f.	Wood Shingles	2,250 s.f.
Sub Flooring	1,534 s.f.	Asphalt Shingles	2,150 s.f.
3½'' Wall Insulation	2,065 s.f.	½'' Gypsum Drywall	7,021 s.f.
6'' Ceiling Insulation	895 s.f.	Ceramic Tile	216 s.f.
1'' x 24'' Slab Insulation	39 l.f.	Vinyl Tile	250 s.f.
Windows (single hung)	19	Oak Flooring	1,010 s.f.
(sliding)	2	Carpet	36 s.y.

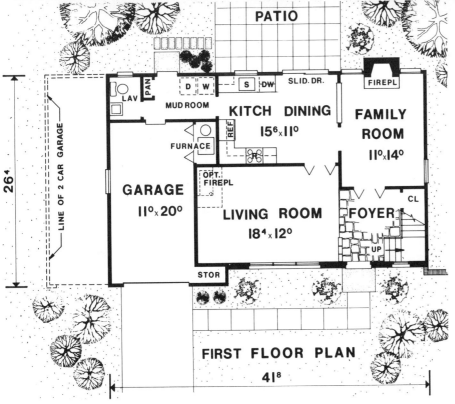

PATIO

LAV | PAN | D | W | S | DW | SLID. DR. | FIREPL

MUD ROOM

KITCH DINING
15⁶x11⁰

FAMILY ROOM
11⁰x14⁰

REF | FURNACE | R

OPT. FIREPL

GARAGE
11⁰x20⁰

LIVING ROOM
18⁴x12⁰

FOYER | CL

UP

STOR

26⁴

LINE OF 2 CAR GARAGE

FIRST FLOOR PLAN

41⁸

THE OAKWOOD

Among the advantages of this very modest, three bedroom, two story home are privacy, a large slate foyer and the economic advantage of building up —which can provide up to 20 per cent more space for the same dollars as a ranch. A careful selection of exterior materials blended into an attractive gambrel roof style gives this home its exterior appeal, while remaining economical to build. A large family room compliments the first floor and features a wood burning fireplace. Many planned "vistas" on the first floor visually expand the otherwise modest space. The second floor can provide for a single large, compartmented, dual entry bath, or two smaller baths.

AREA DATA | First Floor | 790 s.f.
| Second Floor | 666 s.f.
| Opt. Basement | 805 s.f.

MATERIAL LIST

Concrete	(s)	44 c.y.	Doors (exterior)	1
	(b)	74 c.y.	(ext. sliding)	1
Brick Veneer		140 s.f.	(interior swing)	12
Flitch Plates		1	(int. closet)	5
Framing Lumber	(s)	6,787 b.f.	Wood Shingles	1,200 s.f.
	(b)	8,387 b.f.	Asphalt Shingles	1,450 s.f.
Wall Sheathing		1,875 s.f.	½" Gypsum Drywall	6,390 s.f.
Roof Sheathing		1,450 s.f.	Ceramic Tile	301 s.f.
Sub Flooring		640 s.f.	Vinyl Tile	220 s.f.
3½" Wall Insulation		1,000 s.f.	Oak Flooring	520 s.f.
6" Ceiling Insulation		805 s.f.	Carpet	25 s.y.
1" x 24" Slab Insulation		130 l.f.	Slate	72 s.f.
Windows (double hung)		16		
(octagon sash)		1		

DRESS'G

MASTER BED ROOM
15⁴x11⁴

CL | BATH

LIN

CL | CL

DN

BED RM
10⁰x10⁶

OPEN

BED RM
10⁰x9⁶

CL

SECOND FLOOR PLAN

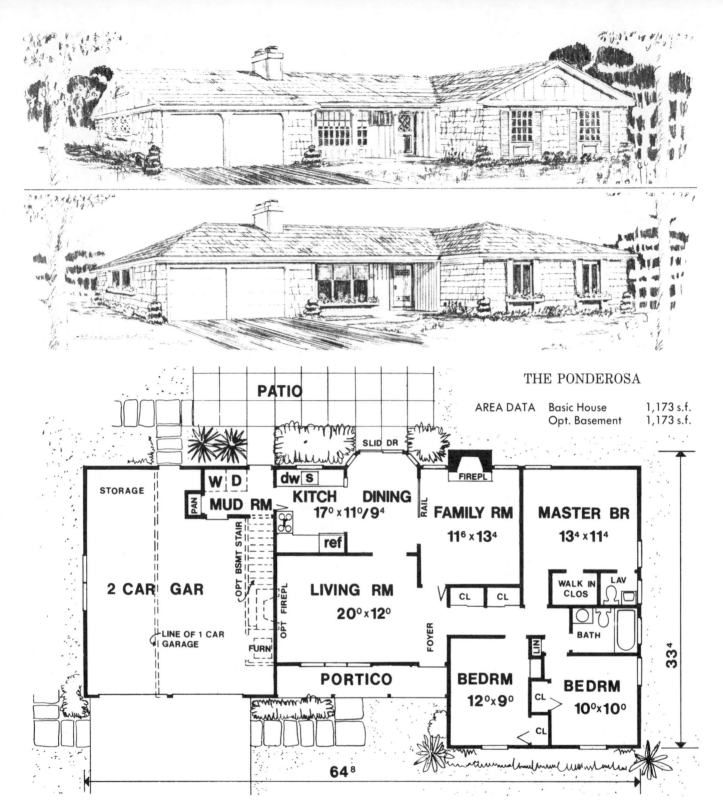

THE PONDEROSA

AREA DATA   Basic House   1,173 s.f.
           Opt. Basement   1,173 s.f.

PATIO

STORAGE

W D

PAN

MUD RM

dw S

KITCH   DINING
$17^0 \times 11^0 / 9^4$

FAMILY RM
$11^6 \times 13^4$

FIREPL

MASTER BR
$13^4 \times 11^4$

WALK IN CLOS   LAV

ref

2 CAR GAR

OPT BSMT STAIR

OPT FIREPL

LIVING RM
$20^0 \times 12^0$

CL   CL

BATH

LINE OF 1 CAR GARAGE

FURN

RAIL

FOYER

LIN

BEDRM
$12^0 \times 9^0$

BEDRM
$10^0 \times 10^0$

PORTICO

CL

CL

CL

33^4

64^8

MATERIAL LIST

Concrete	(s)	44 c.y.	Doors (exterior)	3
	(b)	68 c.y.	(ext. sliding)	1
Framing Lumber	(s)	6,858 b.f.	(interior swing)	9
	(b)	9,072 b.f.	(int. closet)	6
Wall Sheathing		1,670 s.f.	Wood Shingles	1,300 s.f.
Roof Sheathing		2,185 s.f.	Asphalt Shingles	2,200 s.f.
3½″ Wall Insulation		1,300 s.f.	½″ Gypsum Drywall	1,200 s.f.
6″ Ceiling Insulation		1,210 s.f.	Ceramic Tile	93 s.f.
1″ x 24″ Slab Insulation		140 l.f.	Vinyl Tile	180 s.f.
Windows (single hung)		17	Carpet	116 s.y.

This modest sized, three bedroom, seven room ranch house offers a fantastically efficient layout which eliminates wasted space to provide more usable square feet for your dollar. The living, dining and family rooms are laid out for privacy, yet to allow visual enhancement from adjacent rooms through wide openings. The dining area serves as an everyday breakfast room as well as a formal dining area. Although modest, the home does provide most of the amenities of a much larger home, including fireplaces, ample cabinets in the kitchen, a convenient mud room and two full bath units. The home is available in either of two exteriors (the blueprints include both) as well as basement or slab versions.

Choosing a Home Design

Choosing a home design can be a difficult process for some people. The following procedure, though, should simplify decision making. Narrow your choices in three specific areas—size of home, type of home and choice of exterior aesthetic—to make the selection process easy.

Size of Home

This is probably the biggest single factor that determines construction costs. As such you should give it great care. The larger home is usually more lavish: it is also usually more expensive. It can provide all the space you may ever need, but you should ask yourself the question, do you need it all now? If you can do with a smaller home, you can certainly save costs. Also, your choice is not necessarily permanent. You can always add, or remodel, in the future.

This is not to suggest that, if you need two bedrooms now but are fairly certain you will need another one in a year, you should wait and add it then. That wouldn't make sense. If, however, you don't foresee needing another bedroom for six or seven years, it might pay to consider adding it later, providing the home you choose, and your lot, will allow it.

In focusing in on size, first fix the number of bedrooms you need. Then try to determine locally what the construction cost per square foot is in your area. This amount can vary between $20 to $40 per square foot, depending on where you live, whether you will use a contractor, and to some extent on the intricacy of the home design itself. Divide your projected budget for the house (after deducting land, furnishings and landscaping) by this cost per square foot, and you will have a rough guide as to how big a home you should be considering. You may modify this later, but at least it is a starting point.

Type of Home

There are essentially three important house types—ranch, two story, and split level. Each has attributes, and faults.

With a ranch, all the living is on one level. There are usually no stairs to climb, unless the ranch has a garage in the basement, as may be required on certain sloping lots, or as in the case of a raised ranch or split-foyer style of home. It is, however, more expensive to build than a comparably sized two story home (usually an additional 10 to 20 per cent), except in the under 1,400 square foot category, when the ranch may be as economical. The raised ranch is also fairly economical to build.

A two story home has the attribute of greater privacy for the bedrooms than a ranch, as long as you accept the stairs to climb. A ranch lends itself more readily to sloped ceilings, changes in floor levels, and a contemporary character; a two-story doesn't readily lend itself to these design characteristics, although they can be accomplished.

A split level combines the attributes—and deficiencies—of both. The changes in level allow for greater design interest, and provide bedroom privacy. It also readily permits sloped ceilings, and a contemporary character, if desired. But a split level also has stairs, and might require even more up and down movement than a two story. Although more expensive to build than a two story, a split level usually costs less than an equally sized ranch, since it does utilize the economy of multi-level construction in at least half the home.

There are no rules to follow in choosing a type of home, the decision being one of personal preference.

Exterior Aesthetic

As with choosing a type, the decision here rests heavily on personal preference. Preferred styles vary in different localities, although there is a much greater tendency today to accept any style, so long as it is attractive. Of course, if you are building on an historic road, with a certain strong character, it would be wrong to flaunt this precedent. Sometimes there are even deed restrictions regarding exteriors, so check your lot before you buy.

Whatever style you choose, whether it be colonial, Spanish, tudor, contemporary, modern, or something in between, it is important that the house be well designed. A trained architect is aware of certain rules, principles and design guidelines and puts these to use in his designs, whatever the style may be. Changes can be made in these exteriors, but they should be undertaken with guidance. (See section on making changes.)

If you can zero-in on these three criteria—size, type and exterior style—you should be able to find a home design fairly readily.

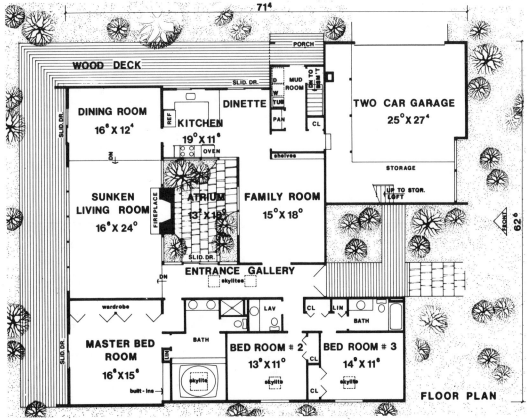

WOOD DECK

DINING ROOM
16⁸ X 12⁴

KITCHEN
19⁰ X 11⁸

DINETTE

PORCH

MUD ROOM

TWO CAR GARAGE
25⁰ X 27⁴

REF

OVEN

SUNKEN
LIVING ROOM
16⁸ X 24⁰

ATRIUM
13' X 18⁰

FAMILY ROOM
15⁰ X 18⁰

FIREPLACE

SLID. DR.

STORAGE

shelves

UP TO STOR.
LOFT

ENTRANCE GALLERY

skylites

wardrobe

LAV

CL LIN

BATH

MASTER BED
ROOM
16⁸ X 15⁸

BATH

BED ROOM # 2
13⁰ X 11⁰

BED ROOM # 3
14⁹ X 11⁸

LIN

skylite

skylite

skylite

built - ins

71⁴

62⁶

FRONT

FLOOR PLAN

THE BERGEN

A large, dynamic, contemporary ranch home focusing around a central atrium. The entrance gallery features a sloped ceiling, as does every room in this home. The conveniently located kitchen and breakfast rooms, and the family room, adjoin the atrium, which can be closed to the foyer. The sunken living room includes a stone fireplace, and along with the dining room faces a rear deck. The master bedroom includes a wardrobe wall and a stunning private bath that features a sunken whirlpool tub. There are also two children's bedrooms, each with a skylite, and another full bath. An oversized two car garage is included, along with an abundance of storage space.

AREA DATA

Living Area	2,550 s.f.

MATERIAL LIST

Concrete	110 c.y.	Doors (exterior)		3
Framing Lumber	21,466 b.f.	(ext. sliding)		4
Wall Sheathing	2,660 s.f.	(interior swing)		9
Roof Sheathing	3,900 s.f.	(int. closet)		11
Sub Flooring	2,640 s.f.	Texture 1-11		2,500 s.f.
3½'' Wall Insulation	2,200 s.f.	Asphalt Shingles		3,900 s.f.
6'' Ceiling Insulation	2,600 s.f.	½'' Gypsum Drywall		8,600 s.f.
Windows (sliding)	3	Ceramic Tile		328 s.f.
(fixed)	24	Vinyl Tile		325 s.f.
		Oak Flooring		1,780 s.f.

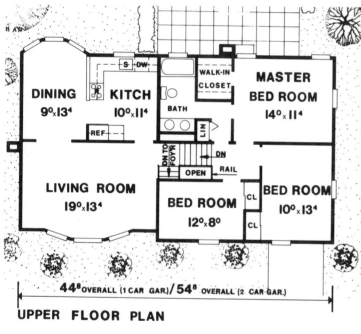

THE BIRCHWOOD

A very modest, yet lovely, split-level home that fosters a much larger impression. The use of different levels in this three bedroom house creates a feeling of great space although effectively zoning various functions and obtaining economies of construction through a compact layout. The lower level reception foyer leads up to the living room, which is designed with an open railing to overlook the foyer. The adjacent kitchen–dining area overlooks the family room in a similar manner. The upper level contains three large bedrooms, an oversized dual entry bath, plus a walk-in closet in the master bedroom.

UPPER FLOOR PLAN

DINING 9⁰x13⁴

KITCH 10⁰x11⁴

WALK-IN CLOSET

MASTER BED ROOM 14⁰x11⁴

BATH

LIVING ROOM 19⁰x13⁴

BED ROOM 12⁰x8⁰

BED ROOM 10⁰x13⁴

44⁸ OVERALL (1 CAR GAR.) / 54⁸ OVERALL (2 CAR GAR.)

25⁸

AREA DATA	Main Level	1,144 s.f.
	Lower Level	357 s.f.
	Basement	420 s.f.

MATERIAL LIST

Concrete	46 c.y.	Doors (exterior)	1
Framing Lumber	9,122 b.f.	(ext. sliding)	1
Wall Sheathing	1,775 s.f.	(interior swing)	13
Roof Sheathing	1,500 s.f.	(int. closet)	4
Sub Flooring	1,160 s.f.	Horizontal Siding	1,120 s.f.
3½″ Wall Insulation	1,540 s.f.	Asphalt Shingles	1,500 s.f.
6″ Ceiling Insulation	1,400 s.f.	½″ Gypsum Drywall	6,750 s.f.
1″ x 24″ Slab Insulation	76 l.f.	Ceramic Tile	282 s.f.
Windows (double hung)	16	Vinyl Tile	385 s.f.
(octagon sash)	1	Oak Flooring	825 s.f.

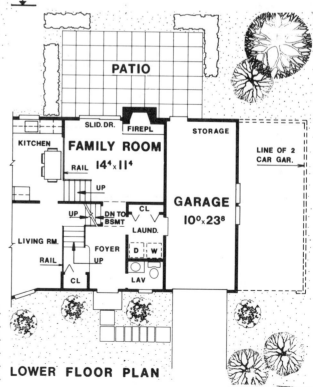

PATIO

SLID. DR. FIREPL

STORAGE

KITCHEN

FAMILY ROOM 14⁴x11⁴

RAIL

LINE OF 2 CAR GAR.

UP

GARAGE 10⁰x23⁸

LIVING RM.

UP

DN TO BSMT

CL

LAUND.

RAIL

FOYER

UP

D W

CL

LAV

LOWER FLOOR PLAN

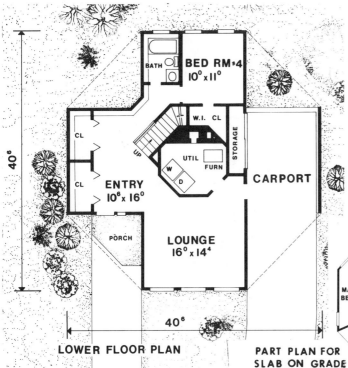

LOWER FLOOR PLAN

PART PLAN FOR SLAB ON GRADE

THE YOSEMITE

A highly dramatic, octagon shaped, contemporary vacation home. Occupying three of the eight sides is the living-dining and kitchen areas, with an abundance of windows, and sliding glass doors opening onto a large covered deck. The ceiling, as in all rooms on the main floor, is sloped. A conversation pit, sunken two steps, with built-in seats and a brick fireplace occupies the center of the home and fixed glass and exhaust fans are up high. A hall, wrapping around the rear of the conversation pit, leads to three bedrooms and two full baths. The home can be built as either a two story, or a less expensive, one story home; either way, the main floor remains essentially the same.

AREA DATA

Main Floor	1,203 s.f.
Opt. Lower Floor	875 s.f.

MATERIAL LIST

Concrete	34 c.y.	Doors (exterior)	1
Framing Lumber	9,648 b.f.	(ext. sliding)	2
Wall Sheathing	2,335 s.f.	(interior swing)	11
Roof Sheathing	1,810 s.f.	(int. closet)	7
Sub Flooring	1,290 s.f.	1 x 6 T&G Siding	1,990 s.f.
3½'' Wall Insulation	2,640 s.f.	Asphalt Shingles	1,900 s.f.
6'' Ceiling Insulation	1,260 s.f.	½'' Gypsum Drywall	7,950 s.f.
1'' x 24'' Slab Insulation	138 l.f.	Ceramic Tile	314 s.f.
Windows (sliding)	19	Vinyl Tile	620 s.f.
(fixed)	5	Oak Flooring	900 s.f.
		Carpet	16 s.y.

MAIN FLOOR PLAN

THE HALSTEAD

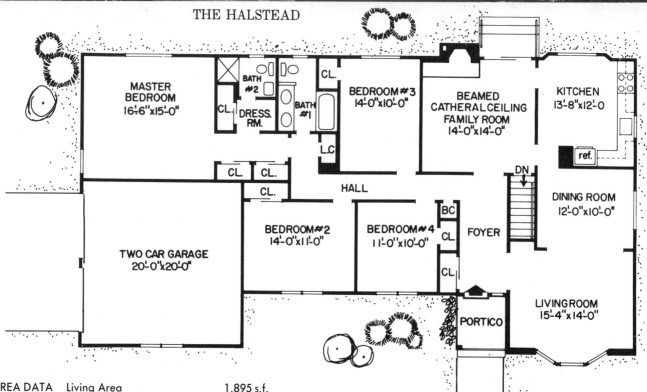

AREA DATA		
Living Area	1,895 s.f.	
Part Basement	480 s.f.	
Opt. Full Basement	1,760 s.f.	
Overall Dimensions	60' x 41'	

MATERIAL LIST

Concrete	(s)	72 c.y.	Windows (alum. single hung)		21
	(b)	85 c.y.	(basement)		3
Brick Veneer		188 s.f.	Doors (exterior)		1
Framing Lumber	(s)	10,425 b.f.	(ext. sliding)		1
	(b)	12,790 b.f.	(interior swing)		11
Wall Sheathing		1,500 s.f.	(int. closet)		5
Roof Sheathing		2,890 s.f.	Wood Shingles		1,280 s.f.
Sub Flooring		530 s.f.	Asphalt Shingles		3,140 s.f.
3½" Wall Insulation		1,625 s.f.	½" Gypsum Drywall		7,305 s.f.
6" Ceiling Insulation		1,705 s.f.	Ceramic Tile		155 s.f.
1" x 24" Slab Insulation		165 l.f.	Vinyl Tile		135 s.f.
1" Rigid Roof Insulation		250 s.f.	Oak Flooring		330 s.f.
			Carpet		135 s.y.

A traditionally styled, four bedroom ranch, of pleasant but not excessive proportions, that is spread out to provide a sprawling, impressive appearance. A covered portico leads to a foyer and center hall that provides ease of circulation to all rooms. The living room features a beautiful bay window, and adjoins the formal dining room. A lovely eat-in kitchen is to the rear and adjoins the family room, which features a plank and beam cathedral ceiling, an optional fireplace and sliding glass doors to the rear patio. The master bedroom includes a dressing room and private bath. Also included are a basement and a side entry two car garage.

THE FAIRLAWN

A charming, yet practical, four bedroom, Dutch gambrel style, two story home. Entry is via an elegant double door to the roomy foyer, with a striking view of the in-line living and dining rooms. A cozy family room with a brick fireplace is adjacent the eat-in kitchen and dinette area, which features a charming three-sided bay window, built-in pantry and planning desk. The mud room adjoins the kitchen. The second floor provides four bedrooms and two full baths. A bonus space is provided over the garage wing, within a matching dutch gambrel roofline. It need not be finished initially, but can be used for expansion. Plans provide for a basement of slab version of the home; either is simple and practical to build.

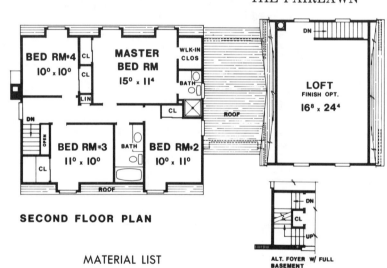

SECOND FLOOR PLAN

ALT. FOYER W/ FULL BASEMENT

AREA DATA	First Floor	969 s.f.
	Second Floor	859 s.f.
	Opt. Loft	433 s.f.
	Opt. Basement	880 s.f.

MATERIAL LIST

Concrete	(s)	45 c.y.
	(b)	71 c.y.
Brick Veneer		175 s.f.
Framing Lumber	(s)	11,423 b.f.
	(b)	13,749 b.f.
Wall Sheathing		2,265 s.f.
Roof Sheathing		2,790 s.f.
Sub Flooring		835 s.f.
3½'' Wall Insulation		1,770 s.f.
6'' Ceiling Insulation		1,120 s.f.
1'' x 24'' Slab Insulation		120 l.f.
Windows (double hung)		21
Doors (exterior)		2
(ext. sliding)		1
(interior swing)		12
(int. closet)		6
Wood Shingles		1,690 s.f.
Asphalt Shingles		2,790 s.f.
½'' Gypsum Drywall		8,990 s.f.
Ceramic Tile		262 s.f.
Vinyl Tile		252 s.f.
Oak Flooring		654 s.f.

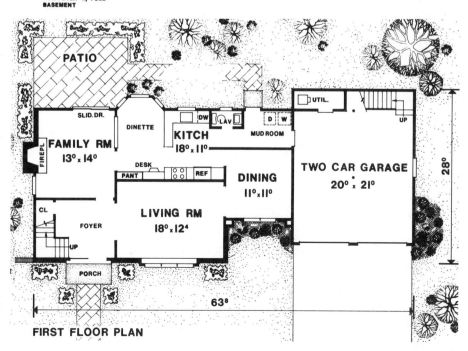

FIRST FLOOR PLAN

THE PIEDMONT

An "upside-down," contemporary split-level home with a soaring dramatic roofline, designed to capture a view. The entrance foyer features a dramatic cathedral ceiling, a skylight and a large expanse of glass facing an outdoor planting area. Also located on this level is a guest room (with fireplace), closets, a full bath and a door to the carport. Stairs lead up to the living area, where cathedral ceilings cover all rooms. The living room includes a main area with large expanses of glass, a smaller, sunken, conversation pit with built-in seats and bookshelves and a brick fireplace wall with a continuous raised hearth. The lower level contains three bedrooms and two full baths. Blueprints include a modest basement or the basementless version.

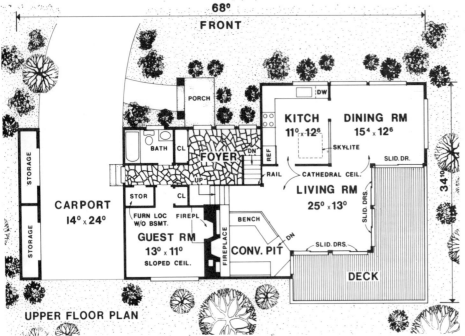

UPPER FLOOR PLAN

AREA DATA	First Floor	1,175 s.f.
	Bedroom Floor	713 s.f.
	Basement	340 s.f.

MATERIAL LIST

Concrete	73 c.y.	Doors (exterior)	2	
Brick Veneer	285 s.f.	(ext. sliding)	6	
Flitch Plate	1	(interior swing)	11	
Framing Lumber	12,112 b.f.	(int. closet)	7	
Wall Sheathing	1,600 s.f.	Texture 1-11	1,850 s.f.	
Roof Sheathing	2,450 s.f.	Asphalt Shingles	2,450 s.f.	
Sub Flooring	1,160 s.f.	½" Gypsum Drywall	6,000 s.f.	
3½" Wall Insulation	2,000 s.f.	Ceramic Tile	459 s.f.	
6" Ceiling Insulation	1,150 s.f.	Vinyl Tile	140 s.f.	
1" x 24" Slab Insulation	95 l.f.	Oak Flooring	615 s.f.	
Windows (sliding)	12	Carpet	80 s.y.	
(oriole)	2	Slate Foyer	130 s.f.	
(fixed)	4			

LOWER FLOOR PLAN

THE DORSET

A rambling, four bedroom ranch of generous proportions, with a charming, early American facade. The living and dining rooms both have a distinctive bayed front. A spacious family room features a cathedral ceiling, a massive brick fireplace with a log bin and an adjacent window seat. The kitchen boasts an abundance of counter space and cabinets, including a center island range and hood. There is also an attractive bay windowed dinette. Adjoining the kitchen is a laundry-mud room and lavatory. There are four bedrooms and a hall bath. The master bedroom includes a walk-in closet, dressing room and shower bath. A half basement is included in the plans.

MATERIAL LIST

Concrete	95 c.y.	Doors (exterior)	2
Stone Veneer	105 s.f.	(ext. sliding)	1
Framing Lumber	14,241 b.f.	(interior swing)	12
Wall Sheathing	2,250 s.f.	(int. closet)	5
Roof Sheathing	3,810 s.f.	Wood Shingles	2,050 s.f.
Sub Flooring	1,105 s.f.	Asphalt Shingles	3,810 s.f.
3½'' Wall Insulation	1,580 s.f.	½'' Gypsum Drywall	8,175 s.f.
6'' Ceiling Insulation	2,420 s.f.	Ceramic Tile	260 s.f.
1'' x 24'' Slab Insulation	120 l.f.	Vinyl Tile	370 s.f.
Windows (single hung)	21	Oak Flooring	880 s.f.
(fixed)	3	Carpet	90 s.y.

AREA DATA

Living Area	2,419 s.f.
Basement	1,029 s.f.

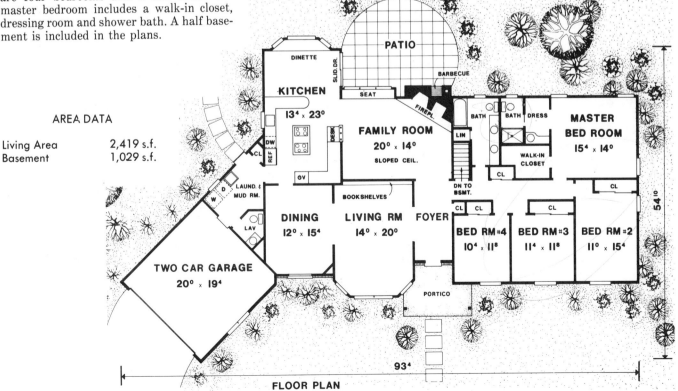

FLOOR PLAN

THE CROWN

A charming, three bedroom, traditional ranch of comfortable square footage, designed to fit a modest lot size. A covered portico leads to an entrance foyer and center hall. To the left is the living–dining room combination featuring a bay window and dramatic angled shape. To the rear of the dining room is a step down, rear entry that provides access to the rear patio and to the family room, with its full brick wall fireplace. The kitchen affords ample work space, and a separate breakfast room. The master bedroom features a walk-in closet, dressing area and private full bath. The home includes an extra deep garage and basement, plus a convenient mud room off the kitchen.

MATERIAL LIST

Concrete	78 c.y.
4'' Stone Veneer	66 s.f.
Framing Lumber	10,213 b.f.
Wall Sheathing	1,977 s.f.
Roof Sheathing	2,420 s.f.
Sub Flooring	750 s.f.
3½'' Wall Insulation	1,727 s.f.
6'' Ceiling Insulation	1,710 s.f.
1'' x 24'' Slab Insulation	104 l.f.
Windows (alum. single hung)	5
(alum. sliding)	4
Doors (exterior)	3
(ext. sliding)	1
(interior swing)	6
(int. closet)	5
Wood Shingles	1,687 s.f.
Asphalt Shingles	2,420 s.f.
½'' Gypsum Drywall	6,580 s.f.
Ceramic Tile	189 s.f.
Vinyl Tile	200 s.f.
Oak Flooring	492 s.f.
Carpet	91 s.y

AREA DATA

Living Area	1,705 s.f.	
Basement	596 s.f.	
Overall Dimensions 52' x 34'		

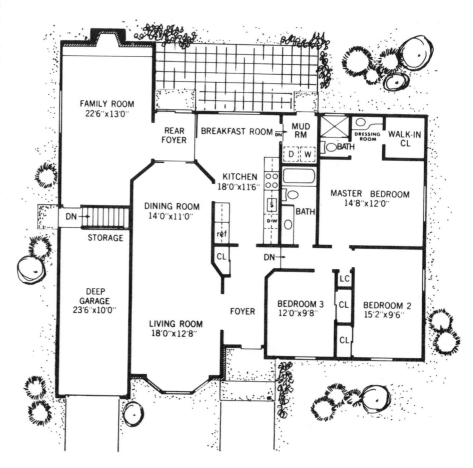

THE ROSEWOOD

This contemporary hi-ranch (bi-level or split-foyer) functions more like a compact ranch, as all major living areas are on the main floor. However, it is even more compact than a ranch, since the garage and utility rooms are located in the basement. The living areas are spacious and dramatic, with cathedral ceilings and sliding glass doors opening onto a wraparound rear deck. The Rosewood also features a large master bedroom with separate bath and walk-in closet. The home is ideally suited for a sloping lot, particularly one that rises up sharply from the street. The basement provides for a large recreation room in the future.

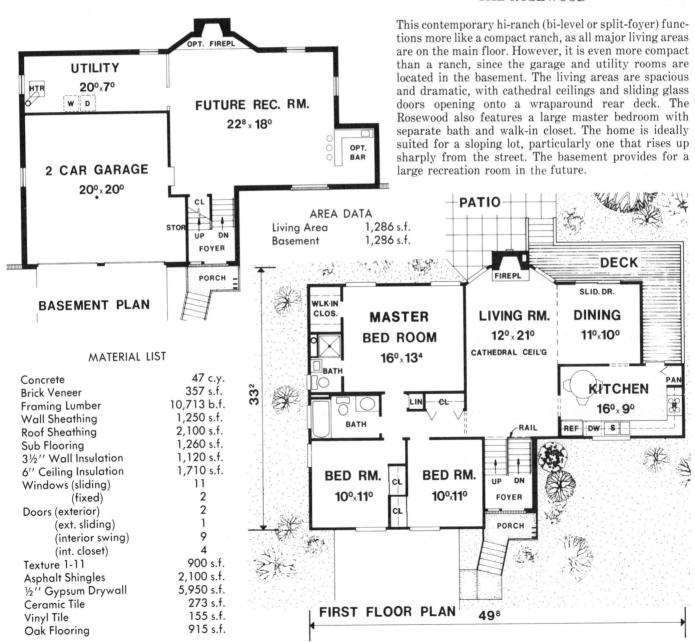

BASEMENT PLAN

OPT. FIREPL

UTILITY
20⁰ x 7⁰

FUTURE REC. RM.
22⁸ x 18⁰

HTR
W D

OPT. BAR

2 CAR GARAGE
20⁰ x 20⁰

CL
STOR
UP DN
FOYER
PORCH

AREA DATA

Living Area   1,286 s.f.
Basement   1,286 s.f.

PATIO

DECK

FIREPL

SLID. DR.

WLK-IN CLOS.

MASTER BED ROOM
16⁰ x 13⁴

LIVING RM.
12⁰ x 21⁰
CATHEDRAL CEIL'G

DINING
11⁰ x 10⁰

BATH

LIN   CL

BATH

PAN

KITCHEN
16⁰ x 9⁰

RAIL

REF   DW   S

33²

BED RM.
10⁰ x 11⁰

CL
CL

BED RM.
10⁰ x 11⁰

UP DN
FOYER

PORCH

FIRST FLOOR PLAN   49⁸

MATERIAL LIST

Concrete	47 c.y.
Brick Veneer	357 s.f.
Framing Lumber	10,713 b.f.
Wall Sheathing	1,250 s.f.
Roof Sheathing	2,100 s.f.
Sub Flooring	1,260 s.f.
3½'' Wall Insulation	1,120 s.f.
6'' Ceiling Insulation	1,710 s.f.
Windows (sliding)	11
(fixed)	2
Doors (exterior)	2
(ext. sliding)	1
(interior swing)	9
(int. closet)	4
Texture 1-11	900 s.f.
Asphalt Shingles	2,100 s.f.
½'' Gypsum Drywall	5,950 s.f.
Ceramic Tile	273 s.f.
Vinyl Tile	155 s.f.
Oak Flooring	915 s.f.

THE MAPLEWOOD

A charmingly traditional, modest sized Cape Cod, or one and one-half story home that provides expansion possibilities. A modest entrance platform is provided just inside the door. It adjoins the living room, which in turn opens, through a wide arch, to the rear dining area. The kitchen is visually open to the dining area, and both rooms open to the adjacent family room, which features a fireplace and large front and rear windows. Two bedrooms and a bath complete the first floor. Although the attic is contemplated as an unfinished shell initially, this space, when finished, provides for two additional bedrooms and a full bath without requiring a front dormer and only a small rear dormer.

MATERIAL LIST

Concrete	(s)	45 c.y.
	(b)	62 c.y.
Framing Lumber	(s)	7,982 b.f.
	(b)	9,568 b.f.
Wall Sheathing		1,850 s.f.
Roof Sheathing		2,250 s.f.
Sub Flooring		150 s.f.
3½'' Wall Insulation		1,250 s.f.
6'' Ceiling Insulation		1,125 s.f.
1'' x 24'' Slab Insulation		140 l.f.
Windows (double hung)		17
(octagon sash)		1
Doors (exterior)		3
(ext. sliding)		1
(interior swing)		8
(int. closet)		3
Wood Shingles		1,670 s.f.
Asphalt Shingles		2,250 s.f.
½'' Gypsum Drywall		3,735 s.f.
Ceramic Tile		88 s.f.
Vinyl Tile		65 s.f.
Carpet		95 s.y.

AREA DATA

Basic House	1,031 s.f.
Opt. Second Floor	571 s.f.
Mud Room & Utility	95 s.f.
Opt. Basement	876 s.f:

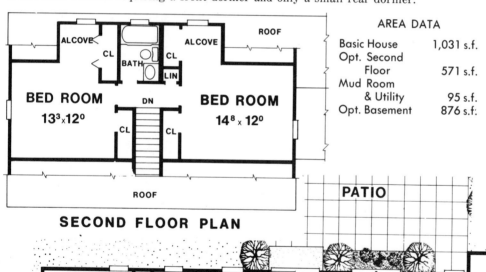

SECOND FLOOR PLAN

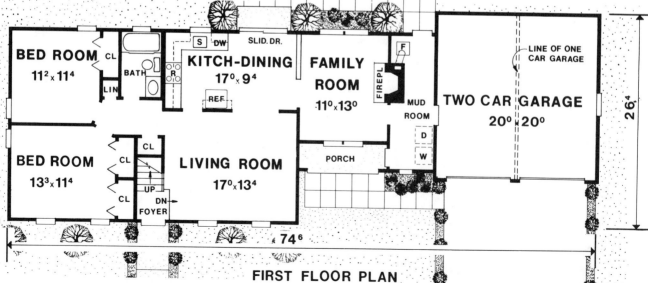

FIRST FLOOR PLAN

THE SHERWOOD

The strikingly dramatic exterior of this Tudor style, split-level home belies its very modest size and practicality. A covered portico leads inside to a modest foyer, which adjoins yet is separate from the front facing living room. A formal dining room overlooks the rear yard and is adjacent to an attractive eat-in kitchen with a charming rear breakfast bay. A spacious adjoining mud room provides ample space for a laundry, sink, sewing area, pantry and closet. The bedroom level includes three bedrooms and a skylit hall bath, plus a walk-in closet and separate full bath in the master bedroom. The family room, located one half flight below the main living level, includes a brick fireplace. The balance can be finished at a later time, providing space for a fourth bedroom or den and third bath.

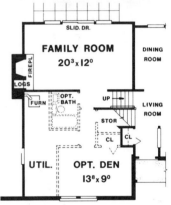

LOWER FLOOR PLAN

AREA DATA

Main Level	1,268 s.f.
Lower Level	266 s.f.

MATERIAL LIST

Concrete	68 c.y.
Brick Veneer	205 s.f.
Framing Lumber	10,468 b.f.
Wall Sheathing	2,150 s.f.
Roof Sheathing	2,630 s.f.
Sub Flooring	700 s.f.
3½'' Wall Insulation	1,450 s.f.
6'' Ceiling Insulation	1,330 s.f.
1'' x 24'' Slab Insulation	104 l.f.
Windows (sliding)	20
Doors (exterior)	2
(ext. sliding)	1
(interior swing)	10
(int. closet)	3
Stucco Panels	1,700 s.f.
Asphalt Shingles	2,650 s.f.
½'' Gypsum Drywall	7,130 s.f.
Ceramic Tile	187 s.f.
Vinyl Tile	470 s.f.
Oak Flooring	500 s.f.
Carpet	55 s.y.

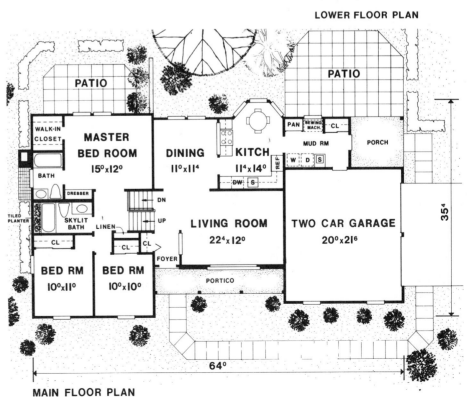

MAIN FLOOR PLAN

THE RAINIER

A four bedroom, contemporary ranch of truly elegant proportions, bursting with excitement and drama inside and out. The reception foyer affords a breathtaking panorama of the sunken living room and balconied dining room. The living room and foyer are covered by a high cathedral ceiling. A stone wall surrounds a two-way fireplace and serves as a backdrop to the living room. The family room, to the rear of the fireplace, features a sunken conversation pit with built-in seats and soaring cathedral ceiling. The kitchen includes a skylight over the center island cooking area, a built-in barbecue and a spacious dinette, topped by a cathedral ceiling. The kitchen adjoins a laundry-sewing room and lavatory. There are four generous sized bedrooms, with the master suite featuring a dynamic bathroom-dressing area. A three-quarter basement is also included.

MATERIAL LIST

Concrete	143 c.y.	Doors (exterior)	2
Brick Veneer	540 s.f.	(ext. sliding)	2
Flitch Plates	1	(interior swing)	14
Framing Lumber	20,183 b.f.	(int. closet)	9
Wall Sheathing	2,020 s.f.	Exterior Siding	1,500 s.f.
Roof Sheathing	4,880 s.f.	Asphalt Shingles	4,880 s.f.
Sub Flooring	2,440 s.f.	½'' Gypsum Drywall	8,930 s.f.
3½'' Wall Insulation	2,070 s.f.	Ceramic Tile	311 s.f.
6'' Ceiling Insulation	3,450 s.f.	Vinyl Tile	500 s.f.
1'' x 24'' Slab Insulation	60 l.f.	Oak Flooring	2,050 s.f.
Windows (sliding)	25		
(fixed)	11		

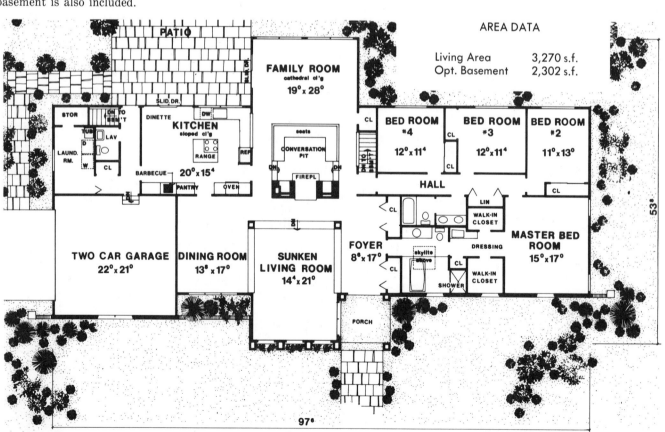

AREA DATA

Living Area 3,270 s.f.
Opt. Basement 2,302 s.f.

FLOOR PLAN

THE SHERWOOD

The strikingly dramatic exterior of this Tudor style, split-level home belies its very modest size and practicality. A covered portico leads inside to a modest foyer, which adjoins yet is separate from the front facing living room. A formal dining room overlooks the rear yard and is adjacent to an attractive eat-in kitchen with a charming rear breakfast bay. A spacious adjoining mud room provides ample space for a laundry, sink, sewing area, pantry and closet. The bedroom level includes three bedrooms and a skylit hall bath, plus a walk-in closet and separate full bath in the master bedroom. The family room, located one half flight below the main living level, includes a brick fireplace. The balance can be finished at a later time, providing space for a fourth bedroom or den and third bath.

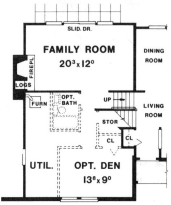

LOWER FLOOR PLAN

AREA DATA

Main Level	1,268 s.f.
Lower Level	266 s.f.

MATERIAL LIST

Concrete	68 c.y.
Brick Veneer	205 s.f.
Framing Lumber	10,468 b.f.
Wall Sheathing	2,150 s.f.
Roof Sheathing	2,630 s.f.
Sub Flooring	700 s.f.
3½'' Wall Insulation	1,450 s.f.
6'' Ceiling Insulation	1,330 s.f.
1'' x 24'' Slab Insulation	104 l.f.
Windows (sliding)	20
Doors (exterior)	2
(ext. sliding)	1
(interior swing)	10
(int. closet)	3
Stucco Panels	1,700 s.f.
Asphalt Shingles	2,650 s.f.
½'' Gypsum Drywall	7,130 s.f.
Ceramic Tile	187 s.f.
Vinyl Tile	470 s.f.
Oak Flooring	500 s.f.
Carpet	55 s.y.

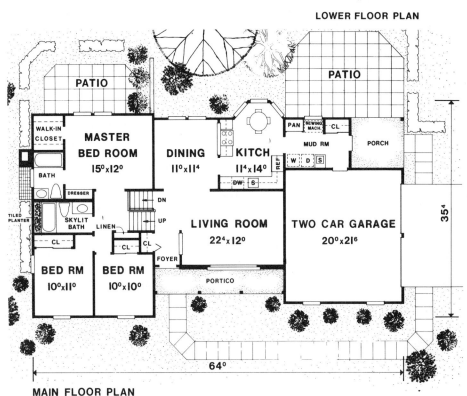

MAIN FLOOR PLAN

THE RAINIER

A four bedroom, contemporary ranch of truly elegant proportions, bursting with excitement and drama inside and out. The reception foyer affords a breathtaking panorama of the sunken living room and balconied dining room. The living room and foyer are covered by a high cathedral ceiling. A stone wall surrounds a two-way fireplace and serves as a backdrop to the living room. The family room, to the rear of the fireplace, features a sunken conversation pit with built-in seats and soaring cathedral ceiling. The kitchen includes a skylight over the center island cooking area, a built-in barbecue and a spacious dinette, topped by a cathedral ceiling. The kitchen adjoins a laundry-sewing room and lavatory. There are four generous sized bedrooms, with the master suite featuring a dynamic bathroom–dressing area. A three-quarter basement is also included.

MATERIAL LIST

Concrete	143 c.y.	Doors (exterior)	2
Brick Veneer	540 s.f.	(ext. sliding)	2
Flitch Plates	1	(interior swing)	14
Framing Lumber	20,183 b.f.	(int. closet)	9
Wall Sheathing	2,020 s.f.	Exterior Siding	1,500 s.f.
Roof Sheathing	4,880 s.f.	Asphalt Shingles	4,880 s.f.
Sub Flooring	2,440 s.f.	½'' Gypsum Drywall	8,930 s.f.
3½'' Wall Insulation	2,070 s.f.	Ceramic Tile	311 s.f.
6'' Ceiling Insulation	3,450 s.f.	Vinyl Tile	500 s.f.
1'' x 24'' Slab Insulation	60 l.f.	Oak Flooring	2,050 s.f.
Windows (sliding)	25		
(fixed)	11		

AREA DATA

Living Area	3,270 s.f.
Opt. Basement	2,302 s.f.

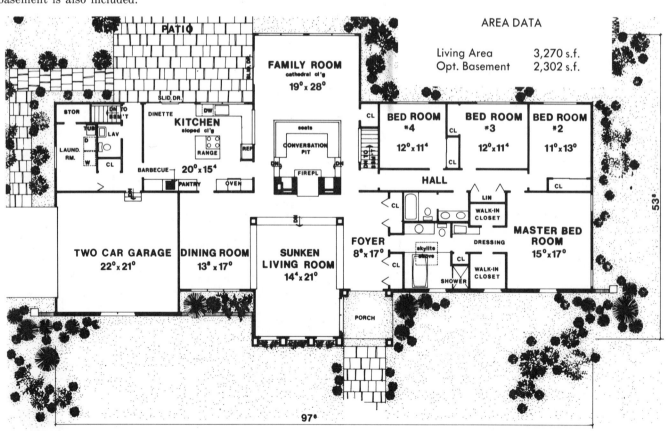

FLOOR PLAN

Choosing a Site

When it comes to choosing a site, there are dozens of considerations including neighborhood, schools, social environment, proximity to churches, and so on that must be weighed. But, since this book is concerned primarily with design concepts, I will assume that you know where you want to live, and are now looking at several lots, and focus particularly on the interrelationship of the home to the site. Here is how to choose a lot, and how to situate a home on it, avoiding at the same time some common mistakes.

Let us review the technical concerns first. Are utilities available (sewer, water, electric, telephone)? If not, how much will it cost to install them? Is the road to the lot improved? If not, how much will this cost? Are the ground conditions suitable (not in a flood plain, too rocky to set a foundation, and so on)? Check out all the title and legal aspects. Are there any zoning restrictions or deed restrictions governing what you can build?

Once the technical concerns are aside, focus on the nature of the lot. Is it a wooded and hilly half acre? If you envision a pool, tennis court and play area, this kind of lot may not be for you. On the other hand, if you are looking at an open and flat two acre meadow, but privacy and minimum maintenance are your goals, this may not be suitable either. So analyze your desires, and see if they will be met on the lot you are considering.

Once these questions are resolved, an all-important one that many people fail to resolve well arises. Will the home I want to build suit the site?

The best way to settle that is to have a home custom designed for you and your particular lot. Since this may not be practical, and you will likely be choosing a pre-designed home, such as one from this book, I have prepared some material to aid you in making the right choice. The diagrams that follow deal with those who already have a pre-set idea about their home—you should review these diagrams as they pertain to the lot you are considering, and see if they require some modification to your choice of home.

Site Shape

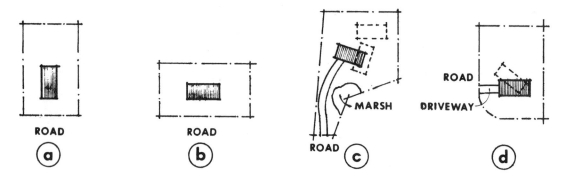

Narrow lots *(a)* may require narrow and deep homes. Check the zoning requirements regarding side yards. Wide shallow lots *(b)* would be best with a wide, shallow home, to leave ample rear yard. Unusually shaped sites, flag lots, and large irregular sites *(c)*, often permit a wide latitude of choices on where to locate the house. They may also allow flexibility to overcome some natural obstacle to building. Placement of the home on a corner lot *(d)* should be such as to permit the most usable rear yard, with maximum privacy. Placing the home so that it faces the shorter road frontage or lies at an angle to the corner is often recommended. The driveway could go to a side entry garage from the opposite road.

Site Orientation

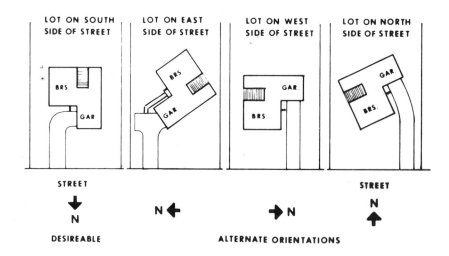

The best orientation, in northern latitudes, is a lot situated on the south side of a street, so that the rear of the home faces south. This allows sunlight to enter the major living areas. There can be negative aspects to this, in summer, if the overhangs aren't large enough to keep out the sun. Since this orientation is found, at best, on only 25 per cent of available sites, it is often not possible to achieve that ideal. However, as the diagrams indicate, often a house can be rotated on a lot to achieve a more desirable orientation. For further information on orientation, see the section on energy conservation.

Site Grade or Slope

Site grading usually causes unnecessary difficulty to the inexperienced builder—and sometimes even to the experienced. Most problems originate from trying to put the "wrong" home on a given site. Unless you are willing to radically modify the existing grade of a lot, the grade is usually the over-riding factor in determining the type of home for the site. Most lots should correspond with one or more of the following diagrams:

Essentially Flat Grade

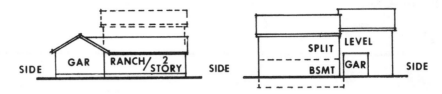

Greatest flexibility, slab or basement, garage can be either side, may need fill for slab.

Not best - basement out of ground.

Grade Slopes Moderately From Side To Side

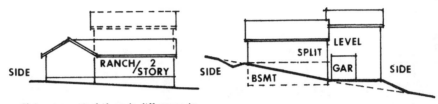

Slab not practical if grade difference is 3 feet or more.

Garage on high side best; if garage on low side, driveway may be too steep and lot difficult to grade.

Fits well with garage on low side.

Grade Slopes Sharply from Side to Side

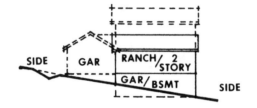

Place a side entry garage under home, in basement. Or, keep garage on grade on high side, and have a walk-out basement on the low side.

Grade Slopes Up From Road

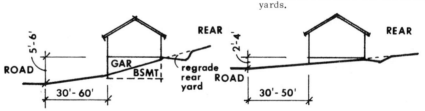

On steep slopes place garage underneath, in front, in basement. Two story home not recommended as it would appear 3 stories high in front.

Regrade rear so water will flow to side yards.

Best arrangement for any ranch or two story, if slope is moderate. Slab or basement.

Grade Slopes Away From Road

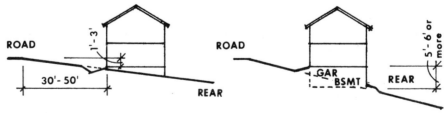

On moderate slope, can erect a ranch or two story with first floor slightly lower than road. Elevation below road can be greater than shown if set back from road is greater. Can be slab or basement.

On steep slopes install walk-out basement at grade in rear. Proper location for garage may be difficult - best location usually side entry into basement.

Many lots are combinations of grades, such as sloping side to side and also away from a road. Follow the suggestions on both grades. It is important to note that construction blueprints can be ordered in reverse, if the grading of the site requires you reverse the home. Also, changes can be made regarding the garage. See the section on making changes.

THE BRIGANTINE

A large, glamorous, three bedroom ranch home with an expansion attic that provides for two additional bedrooms. Upon entering this charming "farm" ranch, the foyer features a cathedral ceiling soaring up to a second floor gallery. An elegant dining room with a distinctive bay window is off the foyer. The spacious kitchen-dinette area is located to the rear, and is adjacent to the dramatic prow-shaped family room with its cathedral ceiling and brick fireplace. A laundry-mud room adjoins the kitchen and provides access to the yard and two car garage. The living room, three bedrooms and two full baths occupy the right side of the home.

AREA DATA

First Floor	2,218 s.f.
Second Floor	676 s.f.
Basement	1,284 s.f.
Overall Dimensions	62' x 50'

MATERIAL LIST

Concrete	91 c.y.	Doors (exterior)	4
Brick Veneer	214 s.f.	(interior swing)	13
Framing Lumber	13,366 b.f.	(int. closet)	3
Wall Sheathing	2,530 s.f.	Wood Shingles	1,270 s.f.
Roof Sheathing	3,440 s.f.	1 x 10 Horiz. Siding	396 s.f.
Sub Flooring	1,310 s.f.	Asphalt Shingles	3,440 s.f.
3½'' Wall Insulation	1,570 s.f.	½'' Gypsum Drywall	7,282 s.f.
6'' Ceiling Insulation	2,220 s.f.	Ceramic Tile	200 s.f.
1'' x 24'' Slab Insulation	72 l.f.	Vinyl Tile	410 s.f.
Windows (single hung)	16	Oak Flooring	830 s.f.
		Carpet	56 s.y.

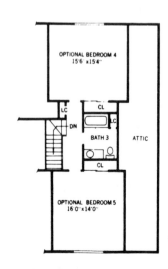

THE HOLLYWOOD

2086586

A striking, contemporary, "California" split-level home with many dramatic features. To start with, there is a raised entrance foyer and an adjacent living room, both with soaring cathedral ceilings. Located four steps down is the cathedral ceilinged dining room, and a kitchen which includes plenty of room for a full-sized breakfast table. Finally, there is the family room with its fireplace, two sets of sliding doors and wet bar. From the foyer, a wide staircase leads to the three bedrooms and hall bath. The master bedroom is no less dramatic with its double door entry, two closets, dressing area, full bath, and sliding glass doors to a private, rear balcony.

AREA DATA	First Floor	1,145 s.f.
	Second Floor	798 s.f.
	Opt. Basement	300 s.f.

FIRST FLOOR PLAN

PATIO

SLID. DR.   SLID. DR.   SLID. DR.   DW

FIREPL

FAMILY ROOM 20⁴ x 13⁰   **KITCHEN** 17⁰ x 10⁰

DINETTE   REF

BAR   FURNACE LOC. W/O BASEMENT   PANTRY

D W   LAV   STOR.   CL   **DINING RM** 13⁰ x 10⁴

MUD ROOM   DN   DN   UP

2 CAR GARAGE 18⁰ x 21⁰   FOY.   CL   RAIL   FIREPL

CATHEDRAL CEIL'G   **LIVING ROOM** 18⁰ x 13⁴

CL

STORAGE   PORCH   PLANT BOX

43⁰

45⁰

SECOND FLOOR PLAN

BALCONY

WALK-IN CLOSET   SLID. DR.

DRESS   **MASTER BED ROOM** 13⁴ x 15⁴

BATH

BATH   LIN   CL

DN

CL

BED RM 10⁰ x 13⁰   **BED RM** 10⁰ x 13⁰

MATERIAL LIST

Concrete	53 c.y.	Doors (exterior)	2
Brick Veneer	270 s.f.	(ext. sliding)	4
Flitch Plates	2	(interior swing)	13
Framing Lumber	11,712 b.f.	(int. closet)	5
Wall Sheathing	2,290 s.f.	Texture 1-11 Siding	1,820 s.f.
Roof Sheathing	2,390 s.f.	Asphalt Shingles	2,400 s.f.
Sub Flooring	1,160 s.f.	½'' Gypsum Drywall	6,800 s.f.
3½'' Wall Insulation	1,950 s.f.	Ceramic Tile	250 s.f.
6'' Ceiling Insulation	1,500 s.f.	Vinyl Tile	516 s.f.
1'' x 24'' Slab Insulation	80 l.f.	Oak Flooring	1,000 s.f.
Windows (sliding)	9	Carpet	17 s.y.

FIRST FLOOR PLAN

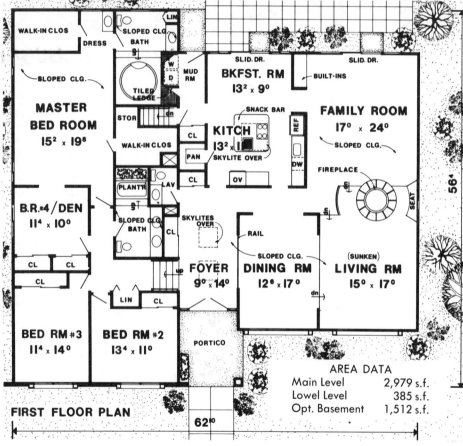

WALK-IN CLOS
DRESS
SLOPED CLG. BATH
LIN

SLOPED CLG.

MASTER
BED ROOM
15² x 19⁸

STOR

WALK-IN CLOS

TILED
LEDGE

W
D

MUD
RM

BKFST. RM
13² x 9⁰

SLID. DR.   SLID. DR.

BUILT-INS

SNACK BAR

FAMILY ROOM
17⁰ x 24⁰

SLOPED CLG.

KITCH
13² x 11

SKYLITE OVER

REF

CL

PAN

CL

OV

DW

FIREPLACE

SEAT

B.R.#4/DEN
11⁴ x 10⁰

PLANTR

LAV

SLOPED CLG.
BATH

CL

SKYLITES
OVER

RAIL

SLOPED CLG.

(SUNKEN)

CL

CL
CL

CL

LIN

CL

FOYER
9⁰ x 14⁰

up

DINING RM
12⁶ x 17⁰

LIVING RM
15⁰ x 17⁰

dn

BED RM #3
11⁴ x 14⁰

BED RM #2
13⁴ x 11⁰

PORTICO

56⁴

62¹⁰

AREA DATA
Main Level   2,979 s.f.
Lowel Level   385 s.f.
Opt. Basement   1,512 s.f.

THE WEDGEWOOD

This large, dramatic, contemporary, split-level home is designed to adapt to a sloping lot yet function inside almost as a ranch home. Sloped ceilings cover virtually the entire home, and there are skylights over the foyer, the second floor baths and the center island of the kitchen as well. A dramatic circular fireplace is located between the family and sunken living rooms. The kitchen also includes a built-in hoodless barbecue, a full window wall and a walk-in pantry. On the lower level, there is a three car garage, a spacious recreation room, a full bath, plus ample utility and storage space. The bedroom level is only four steps above the main level and includes four bedrooms and two luxurious baths. The master bedroom features two walk-in closets, a dressing alcove, sloped ceiling and a bath with an enormous circular tub.

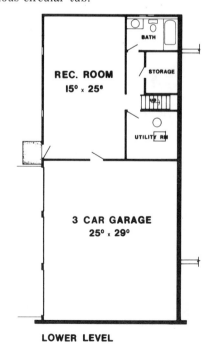

BATH

REC. ROOM
15⁰ x 25⁸

STORAGE

UTILITY RM

3 CAR GARAGE
25⁰ x 29⁰

LOWER LEVEL

MATERIAL LIST

Concrete	(s)	86 c.y.	Doors (exterior)	4
	(b)	99 c.y.	(ext. sliding)	2
Stone Veneer		182 s.f.	(interior swing)	10
Framing Lumber	(s)	14,824 b.f.	(int. closet)	10
	(b)	17,654 b.f.	Cedar Plywood Siding	2,120 s.f.
Wall Sheathing		2,400 s.f.	Asphalt Shingles	3,920 s.f.
Roof Sheathing		3,920 s.f.	½'' Gypsum Drywall	12,330 s.f.
Sub Flooring		1,400 s.f.	Ceramic Tile	574 s.f.
3½'' Wall Insulation		2,000 s.f.	Vinyl Tile	840 s.f.
6'' Ceiling Insulation		3,165 s.f.	Oak Flooring	1,090 s.f.
1'' x 24'' Slab Insulation		120 l.f.	Carpet	124 s.y.
Windows (sliding)		9		
(oriole)		13		
(fixed)		1		

THE NORWOOD

A lovely, colonial style, modest ranch, specifically designed to achieve maximum livability in a home built on a lot that slopes downhill or away from the street. The living room adjoins the entrance foyer and includes a wide floor to ceiling bay window. The kitchen, dining and breakfast rooms face a common trellised deck that overlooks the rear. Accessible from the driveway side and front, as would be required on this type of lot, an un-usual side entry and mud room adds an extra measure of practicality to the design, as does the exterior walkway that connects this side entry directly to the rear deck. A lower level provides for a sumptuous family room, fourth bedroom, full bath, column free side entry, two car garage, and a utility storage area, although these rooms need not be finished in-itially. The finished family room includes a fireplace and sliding doors to the rear.

AREA DATA Main Level   1,395 s.f.
             Lower Level   825 s.f.

MATERIAL LIST

Concrete	53 c.y.
Stone Veneer	58 s.f.
Flitch Plates	2
Framing Lumber	11,581 b.f.
Wall Sheathing	2,080 s.f.
Roof Sheathing	2,040 s.f.
Sub Flooring	1,395 s.f.
3½'' Wall Insulation	1,210 s.f.
6'' Ceiling Insulation	1,860 s.f.
1'' x 24'' Slab Insulation	54 l.f.
Windows (single hung)	15
(octagon sash)	1
Doors (exterior)	2
(ext. sliding)	4
(interior swing)	11
(int. closet)	6
1'' x 12'' Rough Sawn Cedar	1,980 s.f.
Asphalt Shingles	2,100 s.f.
½'' Gypsum Drywall	5,525 s.f.
Ceramic Tile	249 s.f.
Vinyl Tile	290 s.f.
Oak Flooring	980 s.f.

FLOOR PLAN

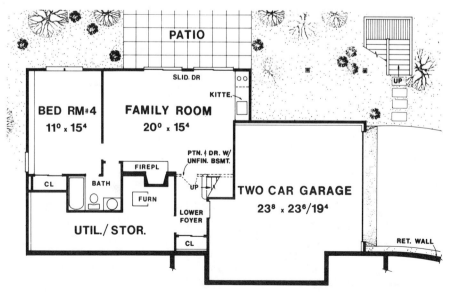

LOWER FLOOR PLAN
FINISH OPTIONAL

THE BARRINGTON

Although the exterior of this distinctive, two story home is a pure, simple, Garrison style, early colonial, the interior is modern and up-to-date. A fabulous 15½ by 23½ foot living room has windows on three sides and sliding doors to the rear patio. Included in the family room are a brick fireplace, built in wet bar and sliding doors to the patio. A spacious U-shaped kitchen and dinette adjoins the family room. The laun-

dry–utility area includes a service entrance from the driveway, and the dinette includes sliding glass doors to the rear patio. The dining room and a spacious two car garage round out the first floor. The second floor includes four bedrooms and two full baths, plus a 35 foot expansion area. The master bedroom features a large, windowed, walk-in closet as well as a full private bath.

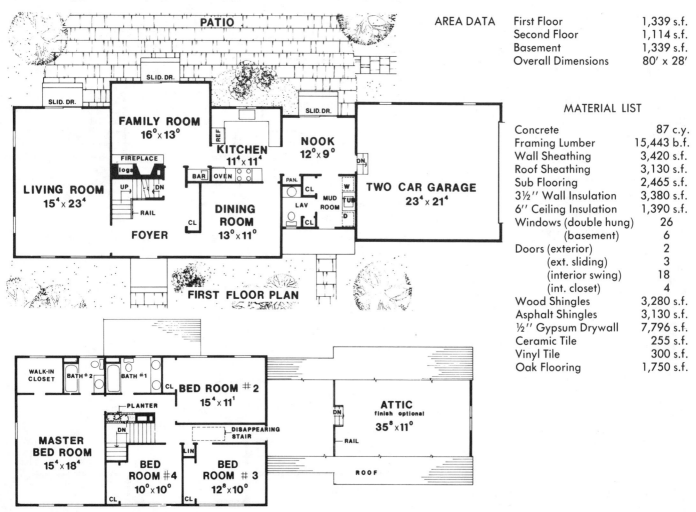

FIRST FLOOR PLAN

SECOND FLOOR PLAN

AREA DATA	
First Floor	1,339 s.f.
Second Floor	1,114 s.f.
Basement	1,339 s.f.
Overall Dimensions	80' x 28'

MATERIAL LIST

Concrete	87 c.y.
Framing Lumber	15,443 b.f.
Wall Sheathing	3,420 s.f.
Roof Sheathing	3,130 s.f.
Sub Flooring	2,465 s.f.
3½'' Wall Insulation	3,380 s.f.
6'' Ceiling Insulation	1,390 s.f.
Windows (double hung)	26
(basement)	6
Doors (exterior)	2
(ext. sliding)	3
(interior swing)	18
(int. closet)	4
Wood Shingles	3,280 s.f.
Asphalt Shingles	3,130 s.f.
½'' Gypsum Drywall	7,796 s.f.
Ceramic Tile	255 s.f.
Vinyl Tile	300 s.f.
Oak Flooring	1,750 s.f.

THE POPLAR

Three broad hip roofs provide distinction to this handsome, three bedroom, contemporary ranch home. Inside, the living room features an attractive two-way fireplace; the dining room adjoins the living room, and the family room is to the rear of the fireplace. Sliding glass doors lead from the family room to a covered porch, and a convenient breakfast bar separates the family room from the U-shaped kitchen, which includes an indoor barbecue adjoining the fireplace. Also included are a laundry-mud room and a lavatory, which adjoin the kitchen, and a two car garage. Plans for both a slab and a full basement are included in the blueprints.

MATERIAL LIST				
Concrete	(s)	60 c.y.	Windows (sliding)	12
	(b)	93 c.y.	Doors (exterior)	2
Brick Veneer		150 s.f.	(ext. sliding)	4
Flitch Plates		2	(interior swing)	10
Framing Lumber	(s)	10,728 b.f.	(int. closet)	7
	(b)	13,706 b.f.	Texture 1-11	1,480 s.f.
Wall Sheathing		1,620 s.f.	Asphalt Shingles	3,300 s.f.
Roof Sheathing		3,240 s.f.	½'' Gypsum Drywall	5,340 s.f.
3½'' Wall Insulation		1,460 s.f.	Ceramic Tile	227 s.f.
6'' Ceiling Insulation		1,550 s.f.	Vinyl Tile	400 s.f.
1'' x 24'' Slab Insulation		166 l.f.	Carpet	98 s.y.

AREA DATA	Living Area	1,547 s.f.
	Opt. Basement	1,427 s.f.

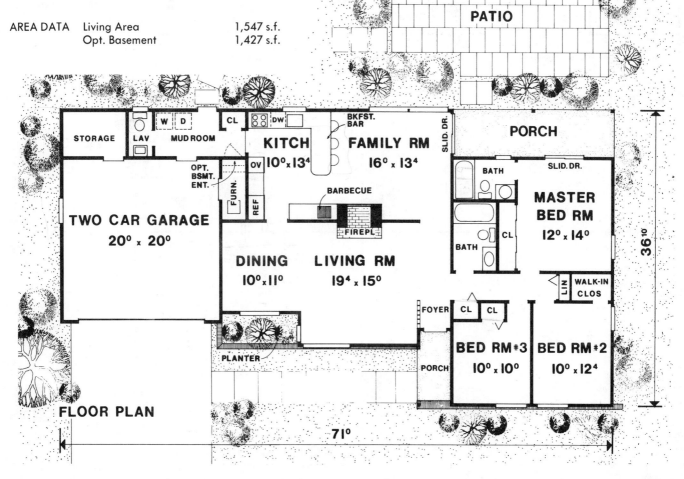

FLOOR PLAN

THE MONARCH

An affordable hi-ranch (bi-level, split-foyer) style home; economical, yet with emphasis on the key elements that make a home desirable. The upper level features an open living-dining-foyer area, giving a feeling of spaciousness. The kitchen includes ample breakfast space and plenty of cabinets and counter top. Three bedrooms and a dual entry bath complete the upper level. The lower level, which initially can be left unfinished, provides space for a second full bath, a fourth bedroom or den and a good sized family room, which features an optional fireplace and sliding glass doors to the rear. A laundry-utility space and a deep two car garage complete this area.

UPPER FLOOR PLAN

| AREA DATA | Upper Floor | 1,056 s.f. |
| | Lower Floor | 541 s.f. |

MATERIAL LIST

Concrete	40 c.y.
Flitch Plates	1
Framing Lumber	7,714 b.f.
Wall Sheathing	2,200 s.f.
Roof Sheathing	1,350 s.f.
Sub Flooring	1,000 s.f.
3½″ Wall Insulation	1,880 s.f.
3½″ Ceiling Insulation	1,530 s.f.
Windows (single hung)	6
(sliding)	5
Doors (exterior)	1
(ext. sliding)	1
(interior swing)	10
(int. closet)	6
Wood Shingles	1,945 s.f.
Asphalt Shingles	1,350 s.f.
½″ Gypsum Drywall	7,990 s.f.
Ceramic Tile	200 s.f.
Vinyl Tile	670 s.f.
Carpet	80 s.y.

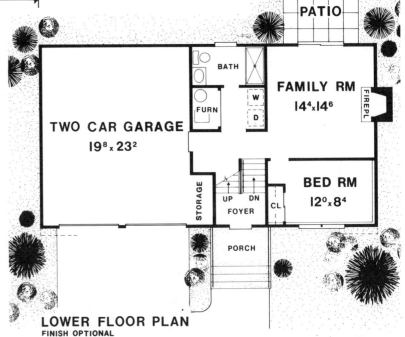

LOWER FLOOR PLAN
FINISH OPTIONAL

MATERIAL LIST

Concrete	(s)	53 c.y.
	(b)	71 c.y.
Flitch Plates		1
Framing Lumber	(s)	8,159 b.f.
	(b)	10,765 b.f.
Wall Sheathing		1,540 s.f.
Roof Sheathing		2,200 s.f.
6" Wall Insulation		1,650 s.f.
12" Ceiling Insulation		840 s.f.
1" x 24" Slab Insulation		144 l.f.
Windows (sliding)		9
(fixed)		4
Doors (exterior)		2
(ext. sliding)		1
(interior swing)		8
(int. closet)		3
Exterior Siding		1,460 s.f.
Asphalt Shingles		2,200 s.f.
½" Gypsum Drywall		4,910 s.f.
Ceramic Tile		118 s.f.
Vinyl Tile		230 s.f.
Carpet		98 s.y.

THE SPRINGSIDE

This strikingly attractive, contemporary, three bedroom ranch home provides gracious entertaining areas for a modest size home. Well suited to any family, it is particularly attractive as a retirement or starter home. A center hall provides access to all rooms and is designed open to the adjacent living-dining room. This spacious room features a cathedral ceiling and a brick fireplace with a raised hearth. To the rear is a highly attractive country kitchen, featuring an extremely efficient U-shaped work area and a cathedral ceilinged dining area; sliding doors lead from here to the rear. The master bedroom includes a walk-in closet and a private shower bath.

AREA DATA

Living Area	1,350 s.f.
Opt. Basement	1,350 s.f.

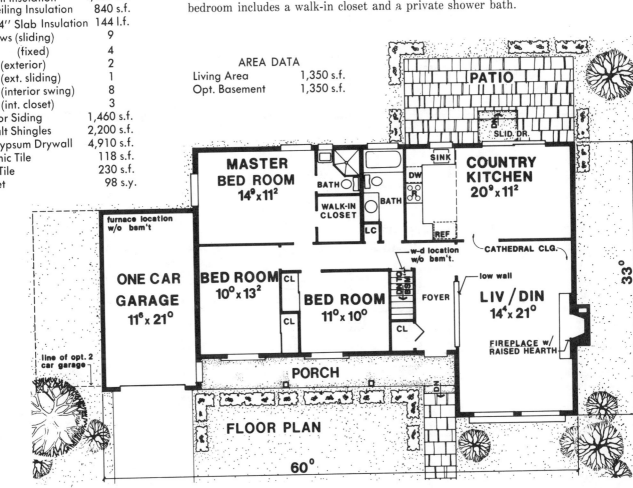

FLOOR PLAN

THE LAKESHORE

A simple, yet attractive, contemporary vacation home that is essentially a ranch that has been raised a full story above ground to enhance views as well as privacy. The upper level includes a living room with a brick fireplace and sliding doors to a screened porch. The dining room opens to the screened porch, as well as to a front balcony. There is also an eat-in kitchen, three bedrooms and two full baths. The lower level includes another two bedrooms, a family room with fireplace and sliding doors to the patio, and a full bath, garage and utility space. If desired, the lower level can be closed to the upper floor, and function as a separate apartment.

AREA DATA
Lower Floor   838 s.f.
Upper Floor   1,204 s.f.

MATERIAL LIST

Concrete	35 c.y.
Framing Lumber	9,460 b.f.
Wall Sheathing	1,575 s.f.
Roof Sheathing	1,734 s.f.
Sub Flooring	1,155 s.f.
3½'' Wall Insulation	2,100 s.f.
6'' Ceiling Insulation	1,304 s.f.
1'' x 24'' Slab Insulation	135 l.f.
Windows (sliding)	12
(fixed)	2
Doors (exterior)	2
(ext. sliding)	4
(interior swing)	14
(int. closet)	5
Texture 1-11	1,624 s.f.
Asphalt Shingles	1,734 s.f.
½'' Gypsum Drywall	7,410 s.f.
Ceramic Tile	338 s.f.
Vinyl Tile	224 s.f.
Oak Flooring	886 s.f.
Carpet	68 s.y.

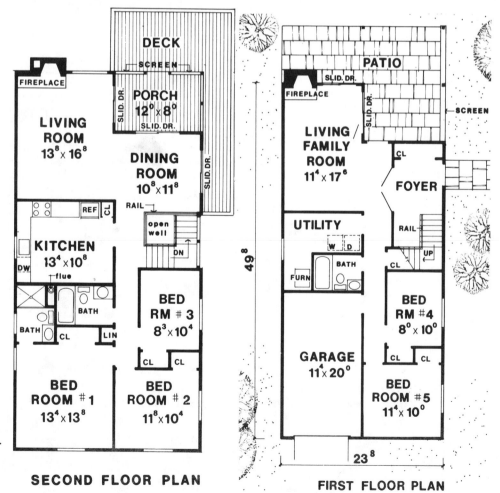

SECOND FLOOR PLAN

FIRST FLOOR PLAN

THE CASCADE

A contemporary multi-level home, designed for a site that slopes steeply toward the rear. The first floor includes the dining room, kitchen and family room, all facing rear, with a window wall in the family room, including sliding glass doors opening onto a deck. Up a few steps is the living room, foyer and an optional den. The living room features a soaring sloped ceiling, a dramatic fireplace, plus sliding doors to a rear deck. The detached side entry, two car garage is located still higher, and serves to create a walled atrium that leads to the slate floored, sloped ceiling, entrance foyer. The uppermost level provides three bedrooms and two full baths. The master bedroom includes a private bath, walk-in closet, dressing room and a private rear balcony.

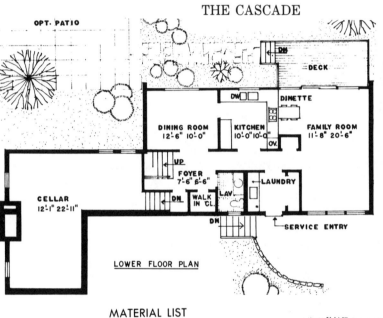

LOWER FLOOR PLAN

AREA DATA	First Floor	872 s.f.
	Second Floor	1,367 s.f.
	Basement	377 s.f.
	Overall Dimensions	69' x 57'

MATERIAL LIST

Concrete	42 c.y.
4'' Conc. Block Veneer	370 s.f.
Flitch Plates	1
Framing Lumber	11,573 b.f.
Wall Sheathing	2,460 s.f.
Roof Sheathing	2,620 s.f.
Sub Flooring	1,300 s.f.
3½'' Wall Insulation	1,860 s.f.
6'' Ceiling Insulation	1,430 s.f.
1'' x 24'' Slab Insulation	110 l.f.
Windows (fixed/awning)	23
(awning)	4
(casement)	4
(fixed)	10
Doors (exterior)	3
(ext. sliding)	3
(interior swing)	13
(int. closet)	8
T & G Vertical Siding	2,210 s.f.
3/4'' Ext. (R.S.) Plywood	120 s.f.
Asphalt Shingles	2,620 s.f.
½'' Gypsum Drywall	6,970 s.f.
Ceramic Tile	210 s.f.
Vinyl Tile	207 s.f.
Carpet	150 s.y.

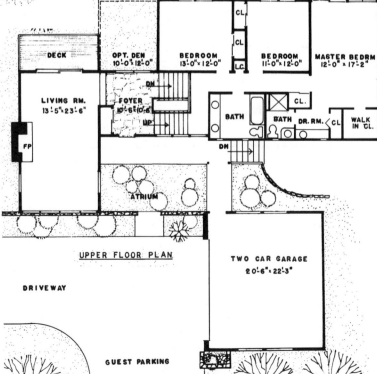

UPPER FLOOR PLAN

Energy Conservation Techniques

As a result of rapidly rising utility costs, all of us have become extremely conscious about conserving energy. In the design and construction of a custom home, this translates into trying to reduce heat loss (and heat gain, as it affects cooling). Such reduction in heat loss or gain reduces the quantity of fuel (electric, gas or oil) needed to heat or cool the home. This saving of energy—and money—can be accomplished in many ways. The following pages detail the various techniques that are available.

The Arkansas Home

The term "Arkansas Home" refers to a home built in accordance with a specific program of energy saving design techniques developed in the late 60s and early 70s in Little Rock, Arkansas. The concept originated as a joint study involving the Little Rock area office of the United States Housing and Urban Development Administration (HUD—also formerly known as FHA) and the Arkansas Power & Light Company.

The developed system, a total one involving all parts of the home, was reported to have produced "incredible savings." As it relied heavily on much larger than usual amounts of insulation, Owens-Corning Fiberglas Corporation became interested. They researched the system and eventually published "The Arkansas Story" which described the details of the system, analyzed the energy savings, and gave the Arkansas Home nationwide prominence.

Following is a list of all the energy-saving features designed into the Arkansas Home, with items keyed to the accompanying diagram.

1. Polyethylene vapor barrier used in conjunction with friction fit batt insulation for walls, floor and ceiling.
2. Double glazing (insulated glass or storm sash). Reduce window area to not exceed 8 per cent of the square footage of the living area.
3. Use of insulated exterior doors with magnetic weather-stripping.
4. Power ventilated attics.
5. Inspection catwalk in attic.
6. Placement of wiring and piping to allow proper insulation placement.
7. Humidifier.
8. Dehumidifier.
9. Electrostatic air filter.
10. Sill and window flashing for brick or masonry walls.
11. Exterior walls—Number 3 grade 2″ x 6″ studs with R-19 insulation friction fit batts.
12. Use of 1/2″ thick plywood headers over windows 40 inches or less in width in place of sheathing.
13. Drop roof trusses squarely over studs to eliminate jacks, cripples and headers, except where openings exceed 24 inches in width.
14. Use of tie plates and drywall back-up clips to reduce number of studs and allow for a single top plate.
15. Installation of ducts within conditioned spaces or use of insulated ducts.
16. Centrally located heating, cooling, plumbing and attic ventilating equipment.
17. Use of 2″ x 3″ studs 24 inches on center for interior partitions.
18. Ceiling—two 6 inch fiberglass friction fit batts of insulation (R-38) with special elevated roof trusses.
19. Crawl space floor—one 6 inch fiberglass friction fit batt (R-19).

DESIGN FEATURES OF THE ARKANSAS ENERGY CONSERVATION HOME

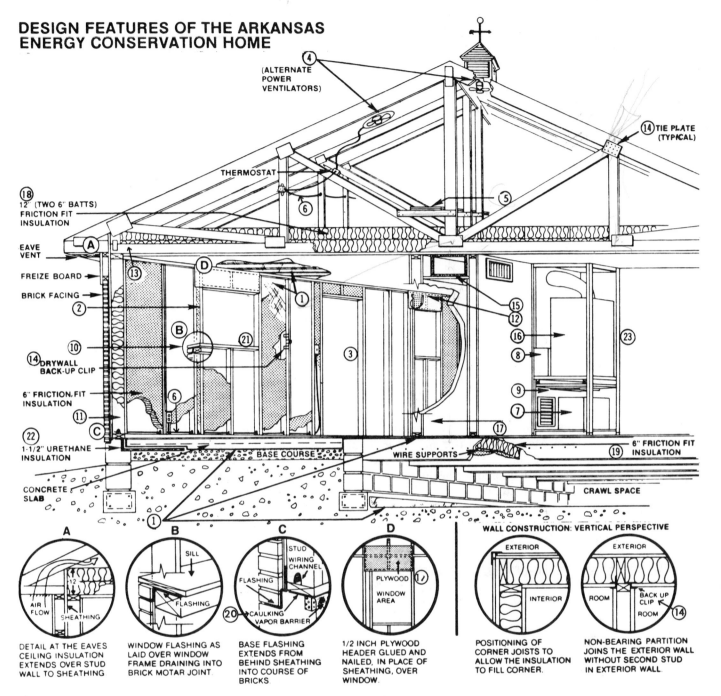

(ALTERNATE POWER VENTILATORS)

④

⑭ TIE PLATE (TYPICAL)

THERMOSTAT

⑤

⑱ 12" (TWO 6" BATTS) FRICTION FIT INSULATION

EAVE VENT

FREIZE BOARD

BRICK FACING

② ⑬

Ⓐ

Ⓓ

①

⑥

⑩ Ⓑ

⑭ DRYWALL BACK-UP CLIP

6" FRICTION FIT INSULATION

⑪ Ⓒ

㉒ 1-1/2" URETHANE INSULATION

CONCRETE SLAB

②① ③

BASE COURSE

WIRE SUPPORTS

⑮ ⑫

⑯ ⑧

⑨ ⑦

⑰

⑲ 6" FRICTION FIT INSULATION

⑳ CRAWL SPACE

㉓

A
DETAIL AT THE EAVES CEILING INSULATION EXTENDS OVER STUD WALL TO SHEATHING

AIR FLOW   SHEATHING

B
SILL
FLASHING
WINDOW FLASHING AS LAID OVER WINDOW FRAME DRAINING INTO BRICK MOTAR JOINT.

C
STUD
WIRING CHANNEL
FLASHING
⑳ CAULKING VAPOR BARRIER
BASE FLASHING EXTENDS FROM BEHIND SHEATHING INTO COURSE OF BRICKS.

D
PLYWOOD
WINDOW AREA
①⑦
1/2 INCH PLYWOOD HEADER GLUED AND NAILED, IN PLACE OF SHEATHING, OVER WINDOW.

WALL CONSTRUCTION: VERTICAL PERSPECTIVE

EXTERIOR
INTERIOR
POSITIONING OF CORNER JOISTS TO ALLOW THE INSULATION TO FILL CORNER.

EXTERIOR
ROOM   BACK UP CLIP   ⑭
ROOM
NON-BEARING PARTITION JOINS THE EXTERIOR WALL WITHOUT SECOND STUD IN EXTERIOR WALL.

20. Sill insulation or caulking around entire perimeter.
21. Drop windows between studs.
22. Concrete slab floor—1½ inches rigid closed cell urethane foam perimeter insulation (R-10.7).
23. Use smaller than normal heating/ventilating/air conditioning system.

The Arkansas Home—An Analysis

Recently, the Technical Services Department of the National Association of Home Builders conducted a thorough evaluation of the energy saving features of the Arkansas Home. Their conclusion: "Although many excellent suggestions are made in the Arkansas Story, it is not necessary that all of the suggestions be used in their entirety and together in order to achieve substantial energy savings."

The heat loss table below, taken from the Arkansas Story, reveals energy-conservation by comparing the loss of heat in British Thermal Units per hour from an energy home and from a typical house—one following the Federal Housing Administration's Minimum Property Standards (now increased substantially because of the incorporation of standards similar to some Arkansas Home features). As can be seen, some of the features which involve modifications to windows and doors, floors, and heating ducts account for a very large percentage of the total energy savings. During construction, these energy saving features can be built-in at relatively little cost.

Heat Loss (BTUs) Comparison Table

Source of Heat Loss	Typical FHA/MPS	Arkansas House	Savings BTUs	Savings Percentage
Window/door	13,131	3,050	10,081	33.2%
Flooring	8,722	3,179	5,543	18.2%
Ceiling	4,320	2,041	2,279	7.5%
Walls	6,757	4,411	2,346	7.7%
Infiltration*	7,548	3,007	4,541	15.0%
Subtotal	40,478	15,688	24,790	81.6%
Heating Duct	6,072	471	5,601	19.4%
Total	46,550	16,159	30,391	100.0%

*total air leakage around windows and doors and from walls, floors and ceilings—difficult to measure.

On the other hand, other items in the table reap relatively small energy savings at what can be substantial cost. Since the energy savings to be expected from each of the different features varies substantially, in order to reap the greatest benefit from your financial investment we stress that each individual construction detail be evaluated separately based on your specific area, climate and cost factors.

Climate and Insulation

The differing climate conditions of the continental United States call for different insulation values. Study the following map and insulation tables for information that will help you to insulate your home for maximum performance.

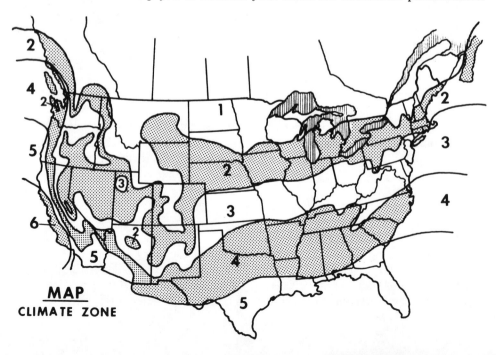

MAP
CLIMATE ZONE

INSULATION VALUES FOR MAXIMUM PERFORMANCE

ZONE	GLAZING	INSULATION CEIL/WL/FL.	CONC. WALL AND EDGE INSULATION
1*	TRIPLE	R-38/19/22	2"
2	DOUBLE	R-33/19/22	1½"
3	DOUBLE	R-30/19/19	1"
4	DOUBLE	R-26/19/13	1"
5	SINGLE	R-26/13/11	¾"
6	SINGLE	R-19/11/11	¾"

* Includes all of Alaska

CEILING:

	WOOL OR FIBERGLASS BATTS	URETHANE FOAM**
R-38	6"+ 6"	5¼"
R-33	3½", 3½", + 3½"	4⅞"
R-30	6"+ 3½"	4¼"
R-26	6"+ 2"	3½"
R-19	6"	2⅝"

WALLS:

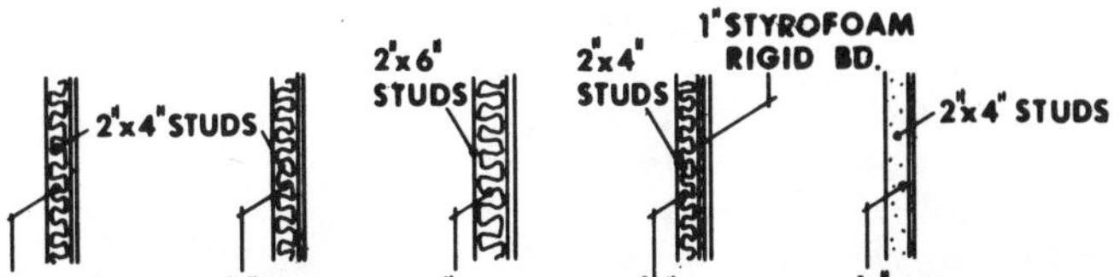
2"x4" STUDS
2"x6" STUDS
2"x4" STUDS
1" STYROFOAM RIGID BD.
2"x4" STUDS

3½" FIBERGL.	3⅝" FIBERGL. OR WOOL	6" FIBERGL.	3½" FIBERGL.	3½" UREA-FORMALDEHYDE FOAM R-19 / 3½" POLYURETHANE FOAM**
R-11	R-13	R-19	R-19	R-24

FLOOR OVER OPTIONAL BASEMENT:

	FIBERGLASS BATTS
R-22	6½"
R-19	6"
R-13	3⅝"
R-11	3½"

Notes: An effective vapor barrier is required on the room side of all R-13 and up insulations using fiberglass. Use foil back gypsumboard or 4 mil. polyethylene.
** Not recommended

8 IMPORTANT ENERGY-SAVING FACTORS

1. Orientation To Sun

Energy Saving Premise: By positioning the home to take best advantage of the orientation of the sun and prevailing winds, reducing windows and openings in the North and West walls and increasing exposures on the south and east walls, we are better able to take advantage of the energy-plus factors that nature provides.

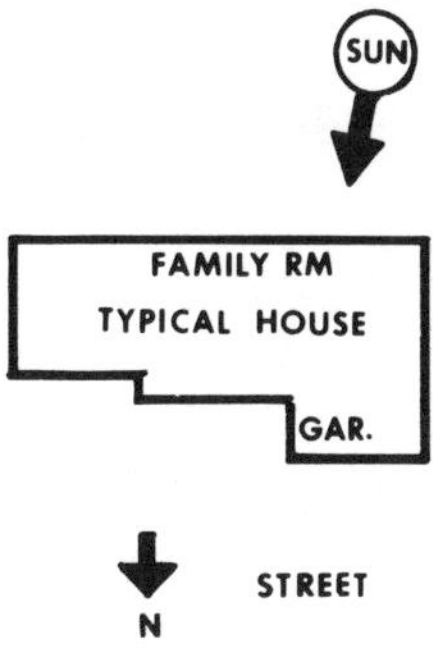
SUN
FAMILY RM
TYPICAL HOUSE
GAR.
STREET
N

PROCEDURE:

If your lot is oriented as shown in the diagram or large enough to allow the home to be angled then follow this procedure. Find true North on your lot. It varies from compass North up to 24° depending on where you live. Inquire of your surveyor. If you live in zones 1, 2 or 3 locate the largest glass areas to face South and locate the garage North, if possible. If you live in zones 4, 5 or 6 and cooling is a major concern you may want to reverse the above. Check with a local heating consultant.

2. Earth Berms

Energy Saving Premise: "Earth berms" rise over three feet on most of the East, West and North side walls. The temperature of these earthen insulators at the floor level of the house is 55° year-round. Thus, in winter, there is only a 15 degree heating differential between ground and room temperature (70°-55°)—not 70°.
In summer, these "earth berms" aid in cooling the house, maintaining the 55° ground temperature and thus helping to dissipate high room temperatures. In addition, they also aid in effectively diminishing the effect of unfavorable winter winds and reduce heat losses on the walls by about 15%.

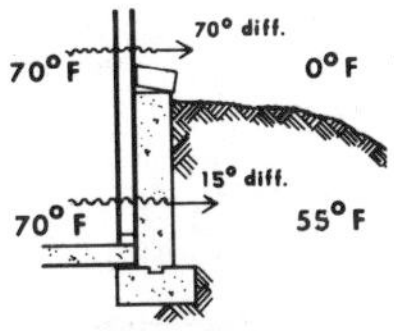
70° diff.
70° F
0° F
15° diff.
70° F
55° F

PROCEDURE:

Recommended for slab-on-grade designed homes only. The top of the foundation walls are raised up 3 feet or so outside the frame wall, and the earth is mounded up against the wall. Of course it must be waterproofed and the footing must extend down to virgin soil.

3. Insulation

Energy Saving Premise: Insulation is one of the most important factors in regulating heat and cold loss. For this reason, higher levels of insulation are used for walls and ceilings.

PROCEDURE:

Locate your home on the climate zone map and read the chart for recommended insulation. The amount saved in respect to the additional cost to achieve these insulation values will vary in each locality depending on local utility and energy costs. If the ceiling or roof construction of your home will not allow the thickness of insulation suggested in the chart, the cost of furring out the rafters, or increasing their dimension, should be weighed against the potential energy savings. Check with your utility company as to what the actual savings will be.

4. Enclosed Foyer

Energy Saving Premise: Another important factor in controlling energy loss is the shielding of the main entry door, providing a closed vestibule inside the main entrance. This aspect of design acts as a deterrent to objectionable temperature and wind conditions. It also serves to keep warmth and cold from being rapidly dissipated by repeated opening and closing of the entryway.

PROCEDURE:

If the plan permits, and aesthetically the foyer can be closed off from all other parts of the home, then consider doing this. Install a door at the inside closed end. Also consider installing an electric heater with a built-in thermostat in the foyer that quickly removes excess cold without turning on the house heating system.

5. Thermal-Break Windows

Energy Saving Premise: Windows are generally poor insulators and act as high infiltration sources for both heat and cold. By carefully locating window openings and choosing a superior grade of "thermal-break" window, we use them to their best advantage as potential solar collectors.

PROCEDURE:

In the climate zone chart find the type of recommended glazing. The term "thermal-break" refers to aluminum windows that have a vinyl separation between inside and outside, thus eliminating condensation problems. Wood windows are, of course, natural thermal-breaks. Investigate various brands of both types of windows, that are distributed in your area, in relation to relative costs, as well as their resistance to infiltration (air leakage). If you want triple glazing, and can't find a window available, you could consider placing storm windows outside of a double glazed window.

6. Trellises

Energy Saving Premise: Summer sun always creates excess heat problems. The fixed wood trellises are used to eliminate virtually all penetration of afternoon sun. They allow the heat from winter sunlight to pass through to the house.

PROCEDURE:

In all climate zones a trellised overhang, over large South facing windows, will allow winter sun through, but block summer sun, while still allowing the maximum penetration of light. The exact angles should be verified with a local consultant. If no sun is desired at all (zone 5 or 6) tinted glass will further reduce heat gain in winter.

7. Hot Water Solar Collector

Energy Saving Premise: Heating costs for hot water can be minimized by adding a unit that will use the power of the sun to generate heat.

PROCEDURE:

The diagram at the left is a typical solar system. There are many variations, though, depending on the manufacturer. Inquire of the various distributers in your area for specifics. In any event the panels should be located on a roof that faces generally South, although it can deviate up to 25° - 30°. The roof pitch should be a minimum of 26° (or 6 on 12 pitch).

Solar space heating is a very involved matter. It should not be undertaken without competent professional advice and design. To install a system on most homes will usually require redesign of the roof as well as the use of the highest possible insulation values.

The four solar heated homes included in this book have been fully engineered. Included with the blueprints on each of these is much additional data on solar space heating.

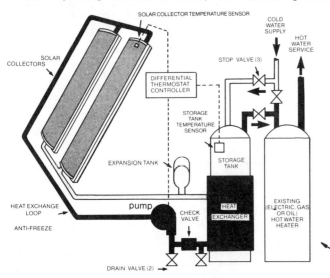

TYPICAL DOMESTIC HOT WATER SYSTEM USING SOLAR COLLECTORS

8. Fireplace Efficiency

Energy Saving Premise: Fireplaces are generally considered negative energy savers because they remove more heat than they create. The 2 fireplaces are fabricated to reverse their negative qualities.

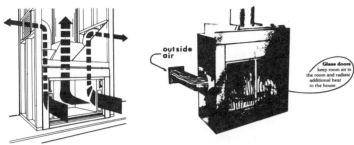

TYPICAL HEAT SAVING FIREPLACES

PROCEDURE:

There are various manufacturers who make several different types of energy-efficient fireplaces. Some are completely pre-fabricated units with metal chimneys. Some are forms to be installed in masonry fireplaces. In either event there are two basic principles to be considered.

The first involves moving air over the heat chamber and circulating it back into the room to make better use of the heat generated by the fire.

The second involves closing the hearth with glass doors and drawing air for combustion from outside, so as not to use heated room air for this purpose.

There are also some products available that utilize the heat of the fireplace to heat hot water in pipes built into the hearth, the hot water then is put to space heating or domestic hot water use.

Suggestions Regarding New Construction

The following comments and suggestions are in addition to the eight important energy saving factors and Arkansas Home features already detailed.

1. Wall and ceiling insulation should be installed with attention to perfection, even in detail work, to obtain maximum effectiveness.
2. Caulk all joints, crevices, sills, and so forth, any place where air could enter the home.
3. Utilize urethane foam core steel exterior doors or solid core wood doors. Use insulated glass glazing in doors. All doors should be well weatherstripped to eliminate infiltration.
4. Provide ventilation of attic by installing a thermostatically controlled roof-mounted exhaust fan. If the roof contains two unconnected attic spaces, install two such fans. Natural attic ventilation will be provided by soffit, wall and ridge vents as indicated on plans.
5. Choose furnaces, air conditioners, and appliances that have high EERs (Energy Efficiency Ratios).
6. If using oil, choose a modern "blue" flame oil burner that operates at higher efficiency.
7. If using gas, choose furnaces and appliances that utilize an electrode ignition system rather than a continuously burning pilot light.
8. Consider zoning of areas and rooms that allow heating (and cooling) of only certain parts of the home at a time.
9. Install a day/night heat control thermostat.
10. Ductwork in unheated spaces should be well insulated.
11. Consider the installation of a chimney stack control device that closes the chimney immediately when the boiler or furnace shuts off. This will prevent heat from escaping up the chimney.
12. Provide an adequate humidifier for winter use.
13. Size heating equipment to real needs—not larger than necessary.
14. Install an outside air cycle device on the air-conditioning system that allows the circulation of cooler outdoor air when conditions permit.
15. Consider devices that reclaim heat from the chimney flue and fireplace flue.
16. Locate air conditioning compressors away from bedrooms if possible and in a place shaded from the sun.
17. Utilize outdoor thermostats to regulate bonnet or boiler temperatures in heat pump and hot water boiler systems.

18. Where dimmer switches are to be installed, utilize solid state dimming switches that actually reduce wattage.
19. Utilize a recirculating range hood in climate zones 1, 2 and 3, and an exhaust fan that exhausts outdoors in zones 4, 5 and 6.
20. Use warm tone roof shingles in climate zones 1, 2 and 3 and light colors in zones 4, 5 and 6.
21. Plant deciduous shade trees on the south side of the home.
22. If there is a good potential for wind power in the locality, consider a windmill to generate electricity.
23. Consider some of the newer, ecologically sound, private sewage disposal systems that produce useful by-products.
24. If the house has a great deal of glass facing south, utilize the passive solar heat gain through these windows during winter days to its fullest. A stone (or similar) floor will serve to "store" the heat for release at night. Insulated draperies or insulated folding shutters should be closed over these windows at night.
25. Consider the installation of storm windows over insulated windows to create triple glazing on certain window exposures (usually north and west) that receive the severest winter onslaught.
26. Insulate all hot water pipes to reduce heat loss.
27. Do not install a domestic hot water tank larger than truly needed and select one with thick insulation on the shell.

Suggestions Regarding Living Patterns

1. Use well fitting draperies around windows, and close them at night.
2. Operate warm-air furnaces with constant fan operation during the heating season to provide more uniform temperatures throughout and eliminate waste of heat. Be sure to have the system *properly* balanced.
3. Shut off lights and appliances when not in use.
4. Change furnace filters once a month during the heating and cooling seasons.
5. Have flue and boiler passages periodically cleaned.
6. During summer cooling it is important that windows be shaded from direct exposure to the sun.
7. Do not open and close exterior doors, or leave them open, more frequently than absolutely necessary.
8. Wash full dishwasher loads only. Shut the dishwasher off at the end of the rinse cycle to save the "dry cycle" and also save energy. Some dishwashers have a control that does this automatically.
9. Taking a shower consumes 50 per cent less water than taking a bath.
10. Use cold water washes and cold water soaps for most of the laundry. Only wash full loads in machines.
11. Use a microwave oven if possible and do not use the self-clean oven cycle more often than absolutely necessary.
12. Make sure the fireplace damper is closed when the fireplace is not in use.
13. Reduce the wattage of light bulbs where possible and utilize energy-saving bulbs.
14. Use fluorescent lamps wherever possible.
15. Consider disconnecting the "instant-on" feature of the television sets in the home.
16. Check to see that refrigerator and freezer gaskets close tightly.
17. Operate energy-intensive appliances in "off peak" hours—usually early morning or late evening.
18. Close off unoccupied rooms and turn off the heat or air conditioning for those areas.
19. Repair all leaky faucets, especially hot water faucets, as quickly as possible.

20. Set thermostat in summer no lower than 78 degrees if house has central air conditioning.
21. Lower thermostat in winter to 68 to 70 degrees during the day and 60 to 64 degrees at night.
22. Reduce thermostat settings when not at home for an extended time.

Your Energy Home

Now that you have read through the foregoing tips and suggestions, you are probably asking, "How do I incorporate all of this into the design of my home?" The answer is simply, you don't! One of the most common potentials for error, in this area of energy conservation, is a tendency to overkill. It is more than likely that many of these ideas, although well intentioned and correct in principle, could cost more than the savings they would generate, even spread over many years.

Since local conditions such as weather, utility cost and construction costs vary so widely, there are no general rules. Equipped with the information here, it would be wise for you to seek out local advice. Contact your local weather bureau, other knowledgeable local officials, heating consultants and subcontractors for their input. Furthermore, your local electric utility company is usually well staffed with personnel informed enough to analyze your needs and answer your questions. Once you have sought and obtained sufficient data, you should be able to make logical conclusions as to which features, and techniques, you want to incorporate into your new home.

Presented on the next six pages are homes which incorporate many of these energy conserving factors. The Centenergy and Dogwood homes are distinctive home plans designed with energy conservation as a paramount concern. The other four homes are solar home designs incorporating heavy insulation standards with solar heating. These four distinctly different homes show how solar heating can be adapted to many "standard" home designs. Construction blueprints ordered on these four homes will also include heating plans, computer printouts and other data on solar heating. These homes can, if you so choose, be built without the solar heating feature.

REAR VIEW OF THE RIVERCREST   **REAR VIEW OF THE HANOVER**

THE HANOVER

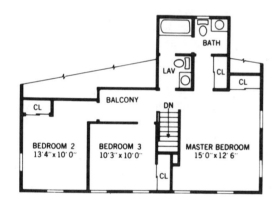

BATH

LAV

CL

CL

BALCONY

DN

CL

BEDROOM 2
13'4" x 10'0"

BEDROOM 3
10'3" x 10'0"

MASTER BEDROOM
15'0" x 12'6"

CL

Although the exterior styling of this modest sized, three bedroom two story suggests a classic salt-box, colonial style home, there is no shortage of contemporary features. First, should you desire it, there is a solar heating system designed for the home. Then, the lovely up-to-date interior includes a foyer flanked by living and dining rooms. The living room connects to the family room, which features a soaring cathedral ceiling, a fireplace, and sliding glass doors to the rear patio. An attractive eat-in kitchen also faces the rear, with an adjoining lavatory and mud room. The second floor provides three bedrooms and one and one-half baths. The second floor balcony hall overlooks the family room below.

AREA DATA	First Floor	1,033 s.f.
	Second Floor	698 s.f.
	Basement	1,033 s.f.
	Overall Dimensions	58' x 28'

MATERIAL LIST

Concrete	60 c.y.
Framing Lumber	10,472 b.f.
Wall Sheathing	475 s.f.
Roof Sheathing	1,840 s.f.
Sub Flooring	1,730 s.f.
3-5/8" Wall Insulation	1,770 s.f.
6" Ceiling Insulation	310 s.f.
12" Ceiling Insulation	750 s.f.
6" Floor Insulation	1,033 s.f.
1" Rigid Wall Insulation	1,875 s.f.
Windows (wd. dbl. hung)	18
Doors (exterior)	2
(ext. sliding)	1
(interior swing)	11
(int. closet)	5
Beveled Wood Siding	2,000 s.f.
Asphalt Shingles	1,840 s.f.
1/2" Gypsum Drywall	5,970 s.f.
Ceramic Tile	165 s.f.
Vinyl Tile	168 s.f.
Oak Flooring	525 s.f.
Carpet	77 s.y.

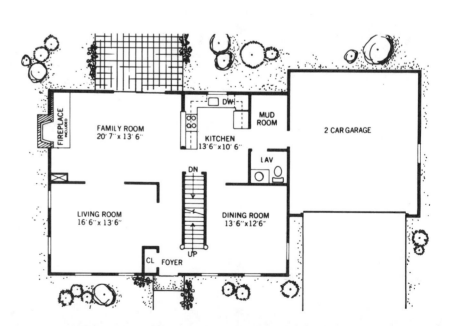

FIREPLACE
INCLUDED

FAMILY ROOM
20'7" x 13'6"

DW

KITCHEN
13'6" x 10'6"

MUD ROOM

2 CAR GARAGE

DN

LAV

LIVING ROOM
16'6" x 13'6"

DINING ROOM
13'6" x 12'6"

UP

CL FOYER

THE RIVERCREST

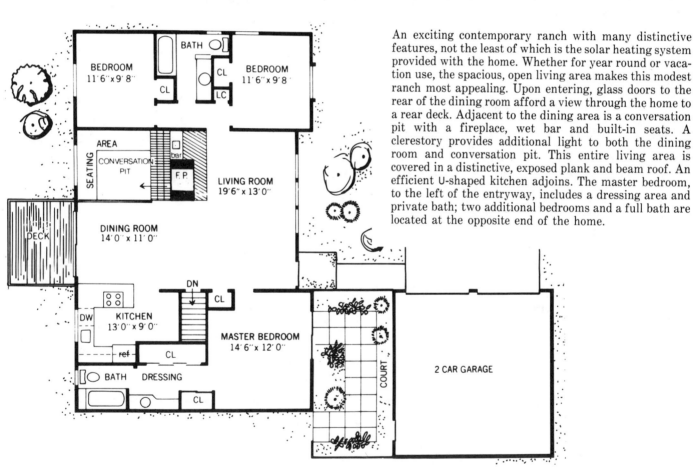

An exciting contemporary ranch with many distinctive features, not the least of which is the solar heating system provided with the home. Whether for year round or vacation use, the spacious, open living area makes this modest ranch most appealing. Upon entering, glass doors to the rear of the dining room afford a view through the home to a rear deck. Adjacent to the dining area is a conversation pit with a fireplace, wet bar and built-in seats. A clerestory provides additional light to both the dining room and conversation pit. This entire living area is covered in a distinctive, exposed plank and beam roof. An efficient U-shaped kitchen adjoins. The master bedroom, to the left of the entryway, includes a dressing area and private bath; two additional bedrooms and a full bath are located at the opposite end of the home.

MATERIAL LIST

Concrete	78 c.y.	Doors (exterior	3
Framing Lumber	13,160 b.f.	(ext. sliding)	3
Roof Sheathing	1,675 s.f.	(interior swing)	10
Sub Flooring	1,320 s.f.	(int. closet)	3
3½'' Wall Insulation	1,200 s.f.	5/8'' Texture 1-11	1,975 s.f.
12'' Ceiling Insulation	810 s.f.	Asphalt Shingles	2,500 s.f.
2'' Rigid Roof Insulation	1,650 s.f.	½'' Gypsum Drywall	4,530 s.f.
1'' Rigid Wall Insulation	1,200 s.f.	Ceramic Tile	214 s.f.
Windows (orioles)	1	Vinyl Tile	98 s.f.
(alum. sliding)	8	Oak Flooring	925 s.f.
(fixed)	5		

AREA DATA		
Living Area	1,351 s.f.
Basement	1,351 s.f.
Overall Dimensions	60' x 52'

THE SARASOTA

This "expansion" or "farm" ranch home has been designed to utilize solar energy, making it as practical as it is attractive. Although modest in size, the home is not lacking in appeal. Upon entering, a small foyer leads to a charming living room which adjoins the kitchen. The kitchen includes a pantry and barbecue. The dining area, separated from the kitchen by a snack bar, features sliding glass doors to the rear patio. Three bedrooms, as well as a dual entry bath, are off a center hall. When completed, the second floor provides two additional bedrooms, a studio with a skylight and a second full bath. Although it is optional, full details on the solar heating system are included with the blueprints.

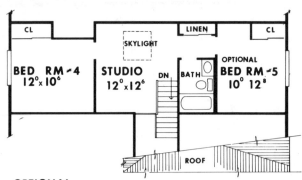

**OPTIONAL
SECOND FLOOR PLAN**

AREA DATA	First Floor	1,187 s.f.
	Second Floor	527 s.f.
	Opt. Basement	1,187 s.f.

MATERIAL LIST

Concrete	(s)	42 c.y.
	(b)	56 c.y.
Brick Veneer		80 s.f.
Framing Lumber	(s)	6,550 b.f.
	(b)	8,431 b.f.
Wall Sheathing		1,350 s.f.
Roof Sheathing		2,150 s.f.
1'' Rigid Styrofoam		1,350 s.f.
6'' Ceiling & Wall Insul.		1,160 s.f.
12'' Ceiling Insulation		680 s.f.
1'' x 24'' Slab Insulation		128 l.f.
Windows (alum. single hung)		11
(basement)		5
Doors (exterior)		1
(ext. sliding)		1
(interior swing)		9
(int. closet)		4
Prefin. Vertical Siding		1,480 s.f.
Asphalt Shingles		2,150 s.f.
½'' Gypsum Drywall		4,540 s.f.
Ceramic Tile		107 s.f.
Vinyl Tile		250 s.f.
Carpet		82 s.y.

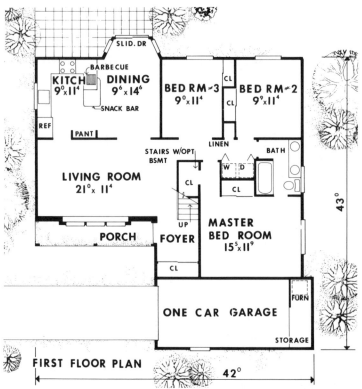

FIRST FLOOR PLAN

THE POINCIANA

MATERIAL LIST

Concrete	(s)	44 c.y.	
	(b)	64 c.y.	
Flitch Plates		1	
Framing Lumber	(s)	8,935 b.f.	
	(b)	11,183 b.f.	
Wall Sheathing		1,270 s.f.	
Roof Sheathing		2,200 s.f.	
Sub Flooring		420 s.f.	
3⅝″ Wall Insulation		1,200 s.f.	
6″ Ceiling Insulation		740 s.f.	
12″ Ceiling Insulation		600 s.f.	

1″ x 24″ Slab Insulation	300 s.f.
1″ Rigid Wall Insulation	1,200 s.f.
Windows (single hung)	4
(fixed)	9
Doors (exterior)	3
(ext. sliding)	7
(int. swing)	6
(int. closet)	5
Texture 1-11	1,180 s.f.
Asphalt Shingles	2,200 s.f.
½″ Gypsum Drywall	5,150 s.f.
Ceramic Tile	292 s.f.
Vinyl Tile	66 s.f.
Carpet	124 s.y.

A rustic, A-frame style vacation home with many exciting features, one of the most stimulating being a solar heating system (a conventional system is also available). The exterior highlight is a prow-shaped living–dining room (its high ceiling being the one concession to energy conservation) featuring four sliding glass doors, a dramatic heat circulating fireplace and outdoor barbecue. Also on the first floor are two bedrooms, an efficient kitchen and a full bath, which includes a six foot whirlpool tub. The second floor provides two bedrooms and a full bath; however, this could be left unfinished initially. The home also includes a second floor balcony, decks, a porch and a garage.

AREA DATA	First Floor	988 s.f.
	Second Floor	450 s.f.
	Opt. Basement	905 s.f.

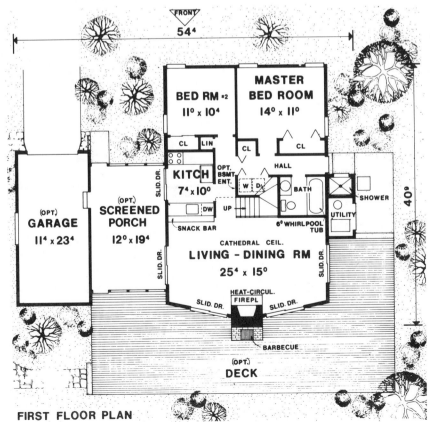

FIRST FLOOR PLAN

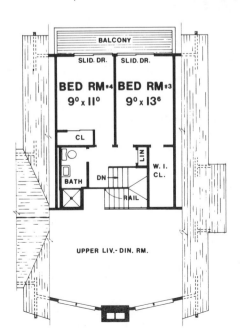

SECOND FLOOR PLAN

THE CENTENERGY

This four bedroom, contemporary, two story home features fourteen energy-saving design techniques —eight important factors are listed in the section on energy conservation. A closed-entry foyer leads to a gallery that runs alongside a plastic roofed atrium, the focal point of the home. Aside from its aesthetic value, this atrium–greenhouse serves to provide passive solar heat to the surrounding rooms. The living–dining room is to the rear of the atrium, an eat-in kitchen to the right. The ceiling of the gallery soars up to the second floor, acting as a summer heat purge. The family room includes a heat circulating fireplace and a cathedral ceiling that conserves heat. The first floor master bedroom suite includes another heat circulating fireplace and luxurious dressing area, which includes a spectacular full bath.

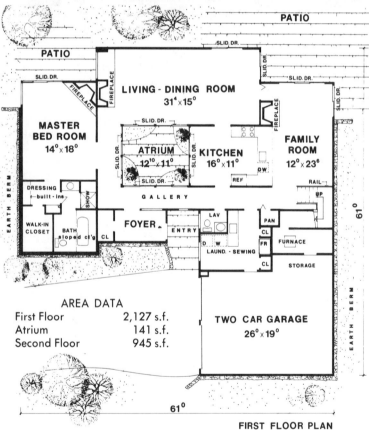

AREA DATA

First Floor	2,127 s.f.
Atrium	141 s.f.
Second Floor	945 s.f.

FIRST FLOOR PLAN

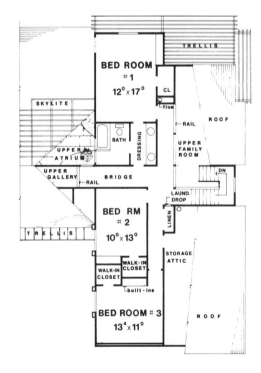

SECOND FLOOR PLAN

MATERIAL LIST

Concrete	74 c.y.	Doors (exterior)	1
Stone Veneer	376 s.f.	(ext. sliding)	11
Framing Lumber	15,779 b.f.	(interior swing)	20
1'' Thick Styrofoam	2,980 s.f.	(int. closet)	4
Roof Sheathing	3,810 s.f.	Texture 1-11 Siding	2,760 s.f.
Sub Flooring	1,180 s.f.	Asphalt Shingles	3,810 s.f.
3½'' Wall Insulation	4,200 s.f.	½'' Gypsum Drywall	10,640 s.f.
6½'' Ceiling Insulation	2,660 s.f.	Ceramic Tile	325 s.f.
1'' x 24'' Slab Insulation	195 l.f.	Vinyl Tile	306 s.f.
Windows (sliding)	9	Oak Flooring	760 s.f.
(fixed)	4	Carpet	144 s.y.

THE DOGWOOD

Innovation is the keyword for this exciting new ranch home. Ten different energy-saving concepts, such as high insulation levels, earth berms, trellis work and proper sun orientation, can work toward saving energy and money. However, these features do not detract from the livability of the home; spacious living areas are centered around a sun-filled atrium, which will bring considerable natural light to this contemporary home's interior. This fully enclosed atrium with its clear roof will serve as a passive solar collector providing energy gain on a year round basis. The plan provides for seven attractive rooms, including a very private living room, a distinct family room adjacent to an eat-in kitchen, a formal dining room, plus three bedrooms and two full baths.

MATERIAL LIST

Concrete	(s)	60 c.y.
	(b)	94 c.y.
Brick Veneer	(s)	64 s.f.
	(b)	532 s.f.
Flitch Plates		1
Framing Lumber	(s)	11,570 b.f.
	(b)	14,824 b.f.
Roof Sheathing		2,880 s.f.
Sub Flooring	(b)	1,660 s.f.
1'' Rigid Wall Insul.		1,220 s.f.
3½'' Wall Insulation		1,220 s.f.
9½'' Ceiling Insulation		1,570 s.f.
1'' x 24'' Slab Insulation		50 l.f.
Windows (sliding)		10
Doors (exterior)		2
(ext. sliding)		8
(interior swing)		10
(int. closet)		7
Texture 1-11		1,280 s.f.
Asphalt Shingles		2,880 s.f.
½'' Gypsum Drywall		6,372 s.f.
Ceramic Tile		292 s.f.
Vinyl Tile		198 s.f.
Carpet		132 s.y.

AREA DATA   Living Area   1,506 s.f.
Opt. Basement   1,466 s.f.

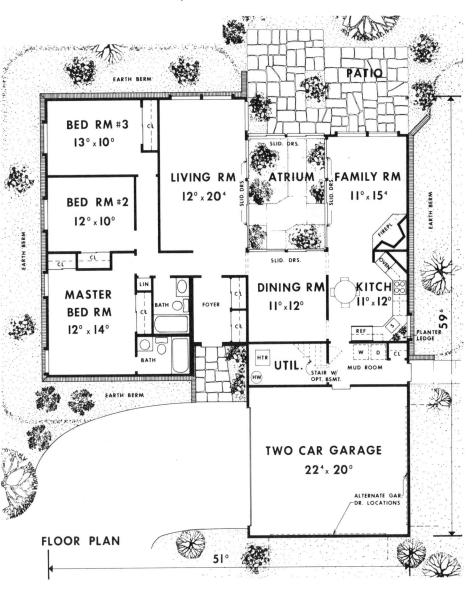

FLOOR PLAN

BED RM #3 13⁰ x 10⁰

BED RM #2 12⁰ x 10⁰

MASTER BED RM 12⁰ x 14⁰

LIVING RM 12⁰ x 20⁴

ATRIUM

FAMILY RM 11⁰ x 15⁴

DINING RM 11⁰ x 12⁰

KITCH 11⁰ x 12⁰

TWO CAR GARAGE 22⁴ x 20⁰

How To Save Money

Anyone building a new home is concerned with the problem of limiting construction costs, and many publications are devoted to that subject. An area often overlooked, however, could have a more fundamental, and substantial, effect on your construction costs. I am referring to making the right initial choices. Decisions about many basic items have a direct relationship to overall costs; yet these design decisions are too often taken for granted, thereby wasting construction dollars.

Decisions and Options

The first and foremost decision you will make affecting costs is the size of the home. This has been discussed previously, but I just want to reiterate that the decision on size in relation to cost is of primary importance.

Next is the area probably best categorized as "options." What I am referring to here are the many items not inherently basic to the home, but added for various reasons; for example, a fireplace. A home *can* be built without a fireplace, but you may not *want* to eliminate it—the choice is yours. Let us pursue this option a little further. A fireplace can cost from $500 for an inexpensive pre-fabricated, free standing unit to $7,000 or more for an enormous stone-faced one with intricate detailing. The choice you make here, too, has a substantial bearing on your total cost. The basis for this and other such option decisions is often as much emotional as it is budgetary.

There is often a third direction, falling between the stark alternatives of "yes" and "no," that you might consider. Again, take the fireplace as an example. It is possible to make certain preparations initially, even if you don't build it immediately, which will enable you to add a fireplace at some future date. This involves merely the addition of a foundation and, possibly, some preparation regarding floor and roof openings if the fireplace will be internally located.

This deferred type of decision suggests a philosophy, that a home should not be regarded as fixed and static, but as something you grow with... something you change, and add to, as you yourself grow. Although this way of thinking may be particularly useful to the younger family, it is an idea that everyone should consider. As with the fireplace, this kind of decision pertains to many other similar options such as air conditioning, appliances, extra bath (leave as a storage closet), expansion attic, rear porch, brick or stone veneer (leave foundation ledge), special gadgets (garage door opening, electronic air cleaner and such), music and intercom systems (do pre-wiring only).

Some options, however, cannot be readily modified later on. These you must address yourself to early, particularly if your budget is tight. For example, if you want a basement, and the home can be built either on a slab or with a basement, you have an important initial choice. Since you would be making history if you succeeded in adding a basement to a slab home, this is a decision—a significant cost decision—you must make before you start. The installation of an outside basement entry or a one or two car garage in a multi-level house are other decisions in this category.

Finishes

After size and options, the choice of finishes is the most significant cost factor in building your home. An inexpensive asbestos tile can cost you 50¢ a square foot in place, whereas an exotic, imported ceramic tile could cost $8 a square foot. Therefore, you have some essential decisions to make concerning the floors, walls, window coverings and light fixtures. Fortunately, you have a little time to make these decisions, because many can be made or changed as necessary, while construction is under way—when you may have a better grasp of your total costs.

Happily, though, decisions in this area are usually the easiest to modify at any time. If you subscribe to the philosophy referred to earlier, you will find making these decisions especially easy. Remember, you can always carpet over an inexpensive tile, install panelling over drywall (which makes it even better), replace a $3 light fixture with a $300 one, and replace inexpensive blinds with built-in shutters. In fact, it is often wiser to defer expensive finishing considerations until after having moved in.

Basic Construction

Finally, your choice of basic construction materials can affect costs, but I do not recommend your tampering in this area. The basic construction of your home should be of good quality materials. Although your kitchen flooring may be inexpensive, you should have a solid underfloor with a thick subfloor, so that you could add quarry tile at a later date if you desire. Similarly, your beams should be of sound quality lumber, and your windows the best quality you can afford. Insulation, sheathing, plumbing, wiring, etc. should also be of good quality—these are not places to skimp. It may not be at all necessary to get the very best, but these are certainly the places to try for second or at least third best.

By following these guidelines, I have no doubt that you can build a home that will be economical and right for you initially, and will ultimately play a large part in your sense of security and belonging.

MASTER BEDROOM
14'6" x 11'6"

WALK-IN-CL

UTILITY

BATH

CL

BEDROOM
13'6" x 9'6"

LC

CL

CL

BEDROOM
10'0" x 9'6"

CL

DW

KITCHEN
14'2" x 11'6"

OPT BSMT STAIR

ref

CATHEDRAL CEILING LIVING ROOM
15'6" x 15'6"

GARAGE

THE BELMONT

A stately porch adds an elegant look to this very modest, traditional ranch home. The home includes a lovely cathedral ceilinged living room with large double windows which create a bright, airy look. A charming eat-in kitchen provides ample cabinet and counter space, plus an attractive dining area in front of sliding glass doors. The utility room is located just off the kitchen. The bedroom wing provides three nice-sized bedrooms and a full bath. There is a walk-in closet in the master bedroom. The extra deep, attached garage provides storage room and an entrance to the kitchen. The home can be built on slab or with a full basement.

AREA DATA

Living Area	1,020 s.f.
Opt. Basement	1,020 s.f.
Overall Dimensions	48' x 27'

MATERIAL LIST

Concrete	(s)	33 c.y.	Windows (alum. single hung)		7
	(b)	51 c.y.	Doors (exterior)		2
Brick Veneer		112 s.f.	(ext. sliding)		1
Framing Lumber	(s)	4,905 b.f.	(interior swing)		9
	(b)	7,114 b.f.	(int. closet)		3
Wall Sheathing		1,420 s.f.	Hardboard		1,200 s.f.
Roof Sheathing		1,590 s.f.	Asphalt Shingles		1,590 s.f.
Sub Flooring (bsmt. only)		1,008 s.f.	½" Gypsum Drywall		4,689 s.f.
3½" Wall Insulation		1,050 s.f.	Ceramic Tile		76 s.f.
6" Ceiling Insulation		1,200 s.f.	Vinyl Tile		172 s.f.
1" x 24" Slab Insulation		132 l.f.	Carpet		72 s.y.

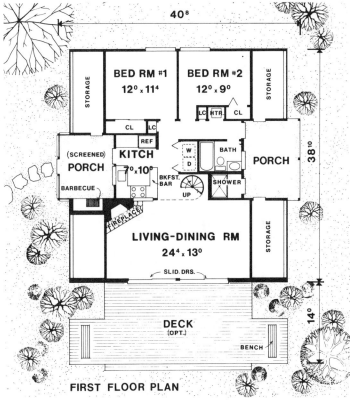

FIRST FLOOR PLAN

- BED RM #1 12⁰ x 11⁴
- BED RM #2 12⁰ x 9⁰
- STORAGE
- (SCREENED) PORCH
- KITCH 7⁰ x 10⁸
- REF
- BATH
- PORCH
- BARBECUE
- BKFST. BAR
- SHOWER
- UP
- FIREPLACE
- LIVING-DINING RM 24⁴ x 13⁰
- STORAGE
- SLID. DRS.
- DECK (OPT.)
- BENCH
- 40⁸
- 38¹⁰
- 14⁰

THE BAYBERRY

Wood siding, stone veneer, decks and plenty of glass add visual appeal to this true A-frame vacation home. A 24 foot living-dining room features a corner stone fireplace, a soaring cathedral ceiling and a window wall of glass, including doors. The efficient U-shaped kitchen is connected to the screened porch, which includes a built-in barbecue—a perfect spot for outdoor dining. A covered service porch, on the opposite side, serves as the ideal all-weather entry and leads to the bedroom hall, off which are two bedrooms and a bath. A stylish circular stair leads to the second floor, which can be finished into a bedroom, walk-in closet and full bath.

AREA DATA   First Floor   924 s.f.
            Second Floor   343 s.f.
            Opt. Basement   1,051 s.f.

MATERIAL LIST

Concrete	(s)	42 c.y.	Doors (exterior)	6
	(b)	53 c.y.	(ext. sliding)	2
Stone Veneer		152 s.f.	(interior swing)	9
Framing Lumber	(s)	6,824 b.f.	(int. closet)	6
	(b)	8,594 b.f.	Texture 1-11	755 s.f.
Wall Sheathing		850 s.f.	Asphalt Shingles	1,850 s.f.
Roof Sheathing		1,845 s.f.	½'' Gypsum Drywall	3,956 s.f.
Sub Flooring		600 s.f.	Ceramic Tile	433 s.f.
3½'' Wall Insulation		430 s.f.	Vinyl Tile	26 s.f.
6'' Ceiling Insulation		930 s.f.	Carpet	104 s.y.
Windows (sliding)		6		
(fixed)		4		

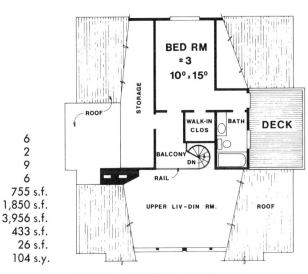

SECOND FLOOR PLAN

- BED RM #3 10⁰ x 15⁰
- STORAGE
- ROOF
- WALK-IN CLOS
- BATH
- DECK
- BALCONY
- DN
- RAIL
- UPPER LIV-DIN RM.
- ROOF

THE COTTONWOOD

A highly attractive, classic L-shaped ranch, but with a few special features. First is an excellent traffic flow pattern that wastes a minimum of space to circulation. Next is the inclusion of four bedrooms; the fourth bedroom could also serve as a sitting room, library, guest room or den. The family room is designed open to the adjacent kitchen, with a breakfast bar between. A two-way brick fireplace is located between the living and family rooms. A modest porch is at the rear of the home. The laundry-mud room, which is adjacent the kitchen, provides a lavatory, closet and access to the rear porch and garage.

MATERIAL LIST

Concrete	(s)	59 c.y.
	(b)	91 c.y.
Brick Veneer		70 s.f.
Framing Lumber	(s)	8,120 b.f.
	(b)	11,440 b.f.
Wall Sheathing		1,800 s.f.
Roof Sheathing		2,800 s.f.
3½'' Wall Insulation		1,550 s.f.
6'' Ceiling Insulation		1,570 s.f.
1'' x 24'' Slab Insulation		157 l.f.
Windows (double hung)		12
(octogonal)		1
Doors (exterior)		3
(ext. sliding)		2
(interior swing)		13
(int. closet)		5
Wood Shingles		1,320 s.f.
1'' x 6'' T & G Siding		170 s.f.
Asphalt Shingles		2,800 s.f.
½'' Gypsum Drywall		5,380 s.f.
Ceramic Tile		374 s.f.
Vinyl Tile		400 s.f.
Carpet		105 s.y.

AREA DATA		
Living Area	1,466 s.f.
Utility–Mud Room	105 s.f.
Opt. Basement	1,475 s.f.

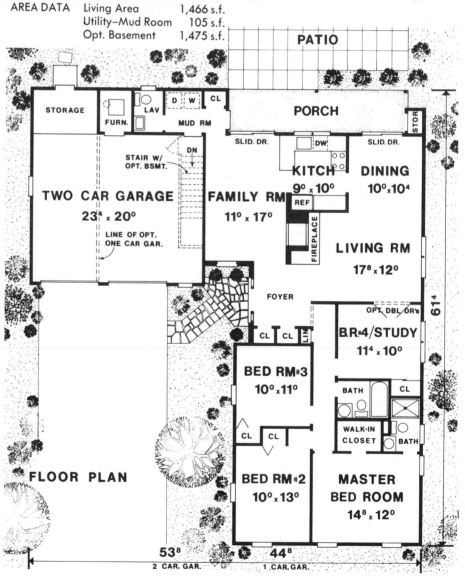

FLOOR PLAN

SECOND FLOOR PLAN

20⁸ OPT MASTER B.R. SUITE   24⁸ BASIC 2ND FLR.

OPT. BATH   BATH

MASTER BED ROOM #1 16⁴x11⁸

OPT. BED ROOM #4 12⁸x16⁸

DN

OPT. WALK-IN CLOSET

LIN   CL   CL   CL

STORAGE

WLK-IN CL

BED RM. #3 10⁰x10⁰   **BED RM. #2** 10⁴x13⁴

LINE OF OPT. 2 CAR GAR.

ROOF

THE JEFFERSON

A distinctively appealing, modest sized, colonial styled, two story home that gives its money's worth in livability. Other adjectives include practical, functional and economical. A sheltered front entry leads to a raised central foyer located between the bay-windowed living room and formal dining room. A dwarf wall separates the kitchen and dinette from the family room, which features a brick fireplace and sliding glass doors. Adjacent to the kitchen is an efficient utility–laundry area. The second floor provides three nice-sized bedrooms, a bath, plus bonus expansion space (376 sq. ft.). Working drawings include plans for an optional two car garage, choice of slab foundation or full basement, and a finished master bedroom suite for the bonus space.

AREA DATA		
	First Floor	877 s.f.
	Second Floor	699 s.f.
	Opt. 4th Bedroom	376 s.f.
	Opt. Basement	960 s.f.

MATERIAL LIST

Concrete	(s)	38 c.y.
	(b)	48 c.y.
Framing Lumber	(s)	8,800 b.f.
	(b)	10,413 b.f.
Wall Sheathing		1,920 s.f.
Roof Sheathing		1,850 s.f.
Sub Flooring		1,080 s.f.
3½'' Wall Insulation		2,073 s.f.
6'' Ceiling Insulation		1,180 s.f.
1'' x 24'' Slab Insulation		120 l.f.
Windows (double hung)		21
Doors (exterior)		2
(ext. sliding)		1
(interior swing)		15
(int. closet)		3
Wood Shingles		1,990 s.f.
Texture 1-11		160 s.f.
Asphalt Shingles		1,850 s.f.
½'' Gypsum Drywall		7,430 s.f.
Ceramic Tile		311 s.f.
Vinyl Tile		240 s.f.
Oak Flooring		900 s.f.
Slate Flooring		35 s.f.
Carpet		62 s.y.

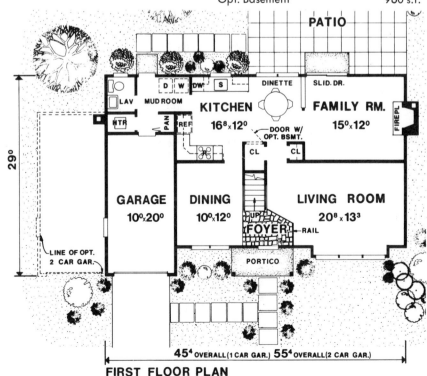

PATIO

D W DW S   DINETTE   SLID. DR.

LAV   MUD ROOM

KITCHEN 16⁸x12⁰   **FAMILY RM.** 15⁰x12⁰   FIREPL

HTR   PAN   REF

DOOR W/ OPT. BSMT.

CL   CL

GARAGE 10⁰x20⁰   **DINING** 10⁰x12⁰   UP   **LIVING ROOM** 20⁸x13³

FOYER   RAIL

LINE OF OPT. 2 CAR GAR.

PORTICO

29⁰

45⁴ OVERALL (1 CAR GAR.)   55⁴ OVERALL (2 CAR GAR.)

FIRST FLOOR PLAN

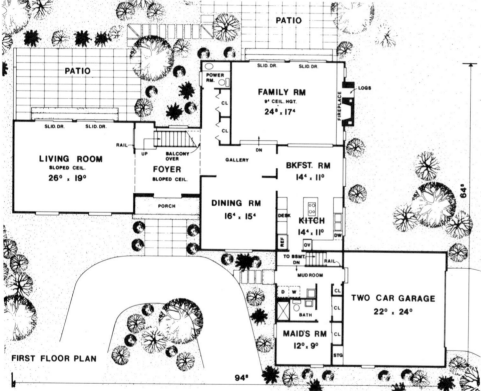

FIRST FLOOR PLAN

Within the floor plan:

PATIO

PATIO

POWER RM.

FAMILY RM
9' CEIL. HGT.
24⁸ x 17⁴

SLID. DR.   SLID. DR.

LOGS

FIREPLACE

CL

CL

LIVING ROOM
sloped ceil.
26⁰ x 19⁰

SLID. DR.   SLID. DR.

RAIL

UP   BALCONY OVER

FOYER
sloped ceil.

GALLERY

DN

BKFST. RM
14⁴ x 11⁰

PORCH

DINING RM
16⁴ x 15⁴

DESK

KITCH
14⁴ x 11⁰

REF   OV   DW

TO BSMT.
DN   RAIL

MUD ROOM

D W

BATH

MAID'S RM
12⁰ x 9⁰

CL

CL

CL

STG

TWO CAR GARAGE
22⁰ x 24⁰

94⁸

64⁸

THE RUTLAND

A lavish contemporary, two story home with a rambling, informal, woodsy appeal. The interior, however, is both formal and dramatic. A sloped ceiling living room and a two-story-high reception foyer, which features a dramatic open stair to the second floor, comprise the left hand, one story wing. The family room, sunken two steps, has a brick fireplace with log bin, and two sets of sliding glass doors. The kitchen includes a center island and adjacent breakfast room. A mud room, maid's or sewing room, full bath and oversized garage are located adjacent to the kitchen, and together comprise the other single story wing. The second floor provides four bedrooms. The master suite features two walk-in closets, a compartmented bath with stall shower, whirlpool tub, bidet and dual basin vanity.

AREA DATA	First Floor	2,381 s.f.
	Second Floor	1,366 s.f.
	Basement	2,021 s.f.

MATERIAL LIST

Concrete	138 c.y.	Doors (exterior)	3
Stone Veneer	126 s.f.	(ext. sliding)	4
Flitch Plates	1	(interior swing)	22
Framing Lumber	24,161 b.f.	(int. closet)	7
Wall Sheathing	5,180 s.f.	1'' x 6'' T & G Siding	4,920 s.f.
Roof Sheathing	3,430 s.f.	Asphalt Shingles	3,430 s.f.
Sub Flooring	3,725 s.f.	½'' Gypsum Drywall	11,300 s.f.
3½'' Wall Insulation	3,270 s.f.	Ceramic Tile	698 s.f.
6'' Ceiling Insulation	2,650 s.f.	Vinyl Tile	460 s.f.
Windows (sliding)	17	Oak Flooring	2,728 s.f.
(casement)	1		
(fixed)	5		

Within the second floor plan:

WALK-IN CLOSET

SLOPED CLG. BATH

WALK-IN CLOSET

MASTER BED ROOM
18⁰ x 15⁸

DN   BALCONY

FOYER

CL

SLOPED CLG. BATH

OPG. W/ STUDY

BED RM #4 /STUDY
14⁴ x 11⁰

CL   CL

BED RM #3
12⁰ x 13⁰

LIN

WLK-IN CLOS

BED RM #2
14⁴ x 12⁰

SECOND FLOOR PLAN

THE AVON

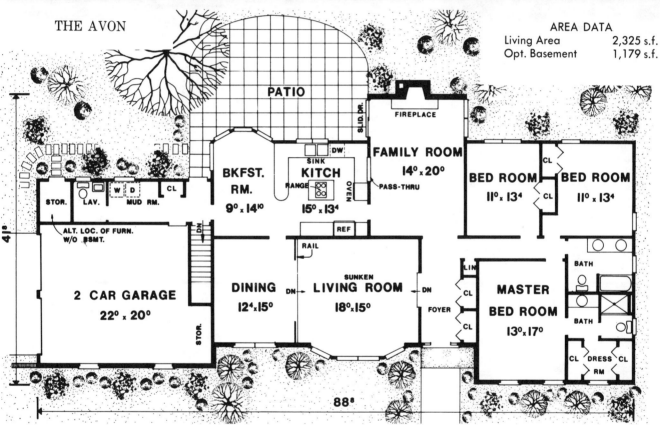

AREA DATA

Living Area   2,325 s.f.
Opt. Basement   1,179 s.f.

Floor plan labels:

PATIO

FIREPLACE

FAMILY ROOM
14⁰ x 20⁰

BKFST. RM.
9⁰ x 14¹⁰

SINK DW KITCH
RANGE 15⁰ x 13⁴
OVEN PASS-THRU

BED ROOM
11⁰ x 13⁴ CL

BED ROOM
11⁰ x 13⁴

STOR. LAV. W D MUD RM. CL

REF

ALT. LOC. OF FURN. W/O BSMT.

RAIL

LIN CL

BATH

2 CAR GARAGE
22⁰ x 20⁰

DINING
12⁴ x 15⁰ DN

SUNKEN LIVING ROOM
18⁰ x 15⁰ DN

FOYER

CL

MASTER BED ROOM
13⁰ x 17⁰

BATH

STOR.

CL DRESS RM CL

88⁸

4⁸

A spacious and attractive, rambling, traditional ranch with a brick front, large windows, and front and rear bays. The living-dining room combination occupies the recessed front area; the sunken living room is separated from the dining room by rails. The family room features a fireplace with a full brick wall, and sliding doors to the patio. The kitchen provides many cabinets, a center island range, and a wraparound bay window in the adjoining breakfast area. The laundry-mud room and a half bath adjoin the kitchen. The three bedrooms are generous in size as is the hall bath. The master suite includes a compartmented bath and dressing room. The home also includes an oversized two car garage and part basement; however, working drawings also show an alternate slab version.

MATERIAL LIST

Concrete	(s)	73 c.y.	Doors (exterior)	2
	(b)	103 c.y.	(ext. sliding)	1
Brick Veneer		515 s.f.	(interior swing)	11
Framing Lumber	(s)	11,529 b.f.	(int. closet)	6
	(b)	13,657 b.f.	Wood Shingles	1,100 s.f.
Wall Sheathing		1,600 s.f.	Asphalt Shingles	3,160 s.f.
Roof Sheathing		3,160 s.f.	½'' Gypsum Drywall	6,700 s.f.
Sub Flooring		1,155 s.f.	Ceramic Tile	312 s.f.
3½'' Wall Insulation		1,360 s.f.	Vinyl Tile	280 s.f.
6'' Ceiling Insulation		2,300 s.f.	Oak Flooring	900 s.f.
1'' x 24'' Slab Insulation		116 l.f.	Carpet	75 s.y.
Windows (double hung)		26	Slate Floor	92 s.f.
(fixed)		1		

THE MONROE

An informal, charming, two story colonial home of generous proportions. It can provide up to five bedrooms, if needed. An arched, covered portico leads to a large entrance foyer opening onto a nine-foot-high family room that features a full brick wall fireplace. Two steps up from the foyer is an ante foyer with twin closets. To the left is a powder room, mud room and two car garage. The kitchen includes a built-in desk, pantry, center island worktop, and dinette space. The second floor includes three bedrooms, a hall bath, plus a lavish master suite. This suite includes a sitting room, with an optional fireplace, two walk-in closets, a dressing alcove and a private bath. If desired, the sitting room could be closed off to function as a fifth bedroom.

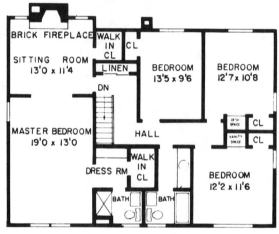

SECOND LEVEL

AREA DATA	First Floor	1,280 s.f.
	Second Floor	1,243 s.f.
	Basement	800 s.f.
	Overall Dimensions	64' x 37'

MATERIAL LIST

Concrete	69 c.y.
Brick Veneer	460 s.f.
Framing Lumber	13,688 b.f.
Wall Sheathing	2,840 s.f.
Roof Sheathing	2,395 s.f.
Sub Flooring	2,040 s.f.
3½'' Wall Insulation	2,010 s.f.
6'' Ceiling Insulation	1,294 s.f.
1'' x 24'' Slab Insulation	46 l.f.
Windows (wd. dbl. hung)	19
(fixed)	1
(bsmt. sash)	4
Doors (exterior)	3
(interior swing)	14
(int. closet)	2
Wood Shingles	2,220 s.f.
Asphalt Shingles	2,395 s.f.
½'' Gypsum Drywall	8,340 s.f.
Ceramic Tile	238 s.f.
Vinyl Tile	227 s.f.
Oak Flooring	1,530 s.f.
Carpet	26 s.y.
Slate Flooring	82 s.f.

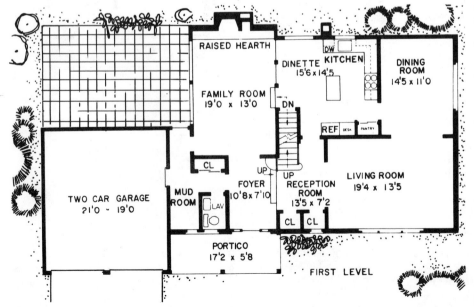

FIRST LEVEL

THE FRASER

An open, functional plan provides for active, informal living in this spacious contemporary ranch. A large front porch and foyer open upon a sunken living room to the right, with sloped ceiling and expansive glass. Behind the brick wall lying straight ahead is a fireplace, the focus of an intimate, sunken conversation pit with built-in seating. The open balconied dining room has direct access to a large, well-equipped kitchen, adjacent to a family room with sliding glass doors to a covered rear porch. Three large bedrooms, two full baths and ample closet and dressing space comprise the bedroom wing.

MATERIAL LIST

Concrete	(s)	77 c.y.	Doors (exterior)	4
	(b)	107 c.y.	(ext. sliding)	3
Flitch Plate		1	(interior swing)	15
Framing Lumber	(s)	11,506 b.f.	(int. closet)	5
	(b)	15,899 b.f.	Texture 1-11	1,930 s.f.
Wall Sheathing		2,080 s.f.	Asphalt Shingles	4,150 s.f.
Roof Sheathing		4,150 s.f.	½" Gypsum Drywall	5,710 s.f.
3½" Wall Insulation		1,280 s.f.	Ceramic Tile	276 s.f.
6" Ceiling Insulation		2,095 s.f.	Vinyl Tile	280 s.f.
1" x 24" Slab Insulation		220 l.f.	Carpet	180 s.y.
Windows (awning)		14		
(casement)		1		

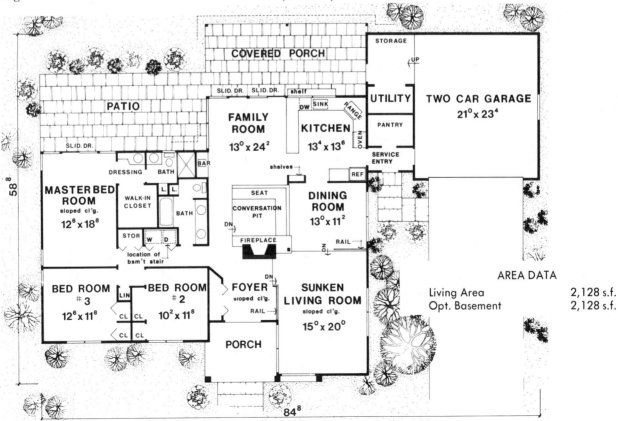

AREA DATA

Living Area	2,128 s.f.
Opt. Basement	2,128 s.f.

FLOOR PLAN

AREA DATA First Floor   1,375 s.f.
           Second Floor   896 s.f.
           Opt. Basement   1,299 s.f.

THE MONMOUTH

The clarity and simplicity of this salt-box style, two story home has been retained, while providing for a modern attractive interior. The first floor affords a spacious living room and a comfortable dining room. The large, partially cathedral ceilinged family room includes a fireplace, game storage closet and access to both the patio and the breezeway connecting the garage. The efficient U-shaped kitchen includes a breakfast bar. A den, or spare bedroom, is located off the entrance foyer. The second floor provides for three generous-sized bedrooms and two full baths. A modest sitting room, off the master bedroom, includes a fireplace and overlooks the family room.

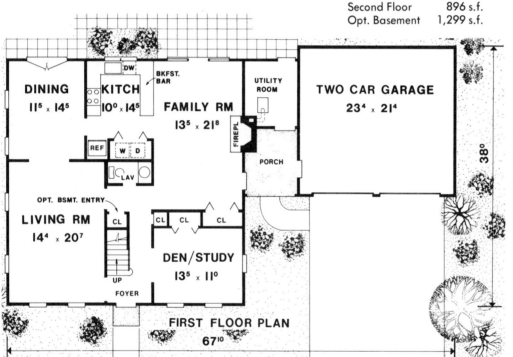

FIRST FLOOR PLAN

MATERIAL LIST

Concrete	(s)	54 c.y.	Doors (exterior)	8
	(b)	78 c.y.	(interior swing)	15
Framing Lumber	(s)	10,950 b.f.	(int. closet)	4
	(b)	12,992 b.f.	Exterior Siding	3,800 s.f.
Wall Sheathing		3,820 s.f.	Asphalt Shingles	2,680 s.f.
Roof Sheathing		2,680 s.f.	½'' Gypsum Drywall	7,380 s.f.
Sub Flooring		1,274 s.f.	Ceramic Tile	236 s.f.
3½'' Wall Insulation		1,820 s.f.	Vinyl Tile	144 s.f.
6'' Ceiling Insulation		1,380 s.f.	Oak Flooring	700 s.f.
1'' x 24'' Slab Insulation		124 l.f.	Carpet	112 s.y.
Windows (double hung)		23		

SECOND FLOOR PLAN

THE SCOTCHWOOD

A triple tier roof and attractive front portico distinguish this charming three bedroom, traditional ranch home. Inside, the home is compact and economical, yet it contains many spaces which are suited to active family life. The living room features a cathedral ceiling and brick fireplace. Just beyond is the family room, a relaxing room which includes a built-in bar and sliding glass doors to a patio. The spacious kitchen beyond overlooks the dining area which, due to its circular shape and wraparound windows, will be filled with natural light most of the day.

AREA DATA Living Area   1,396 s.f.
          Opt. Basement   812 s.f.

MATERIAL LIST

Concrete	(s)	54 c.y.	Doors (exterior)	2
	(b)	79 c.y.	(ext. sliding)	1
Brick Veneer		180 s.f.	(interior swing)	10
Framing Lumber	(s)	6,940 b.f.	(int. closet)	5
	(b)	8,953 b.f.	Texture 1-11	1,300 s.f.
Wall Sheathing		250 s.f.	Asphalt Shingles	2,300 s.f.
Roof Sheathing		2,275 s.f.	½'' Gypsum Drywall	5,870 s.f.
3½'' Wall Insulation		1,432 s.f.	Ceramic Tile	223 s.f.
6'' Ceiling Insulation		1,400 s.f.	Vinyl Tile	320 s.f.
1'' x 24'' Slab Insulation		300 l.f.	Oak Tiles	430 s.f.
Windows (single hung)		17	Carpet	54 s.y.
(sliding)		2		

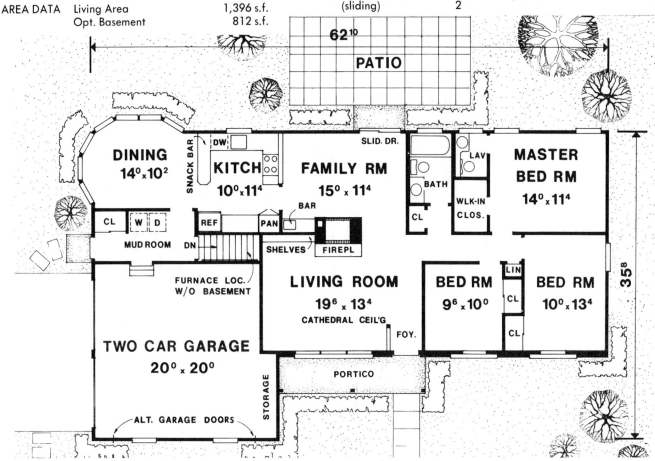

THE ALPINE

A dramatic, contemporary, two story home with sloped ceilings throughout and separate bedrooms on two floors, for year around or vacation use. A tall covered porch leads to the cathedral ceilinged entrance foyer and a panoramic view of the interior. The sunken living room includes large corner windows and a brick fireplace. A sloped ceiling dining room, efficient U-shaped kitchen and adjoining breakfast room with sliding glass doors are all to the rear. The laundry–mud room and pantry adjoin the breakfast room. A bedroom and full bath complete the first floor. The second floor includes two sloped ceiling bedrooms, plenty of closets and another full bath. Blueprints include plans for the optional two car garage.

FIRST FLOOR PLAN

PATIO

(OPTIONAL) **TWO CAR GARAGE** 22⁰ x 20⁰

SLOPED CEIL. **DINING** 11⁰ x 10⁶

KITCH 10⁶ x 10⁶

BKFST. RM 11⁰ x 9⁰

FURNACE

LAUND. RM.

FIREPL (SUNKEN) **LIVING RM** 18⁰ x 12⁰ SLOPED CEIL.

DN REF

PANTRY

BATH

UP OPT. BSMT. ENTRY

FOYER

BED ROOM #1 14⁴ x 11⁰

PORCH

40⁸

23⁶ 8⁰

AREA DATA
First Floor 1,100 s.f.
Second Floor 600 s.f.
Opt. Basement 1,060 s.f.

SECOND FLOOR PLAN

DECK ROOF

SLID. DR.

CLOSET

BED ROOM #3 18⁴ x 9⁰/12⁰

LIN CLOSET

UPPER FOYER

DN RAIL

BATH

CLOSET

SLOPED CEIL. **BED ROOM #2** 14⁴ x 11⁰

SLID. DR.

DECK

MATERIAL LIST

Concrete	(s)	47 c.y.	Doors (exterior)	2
	(b)	72 c.y.	(ext. sliding)	3
Framing Lumber	(s)	8,998 b.f.	(interior swing)	12
	(b)	11,113 b.f.	(int. closet)	6
Wall Sheathing		2,000 s.f.	Texture 1-11 Siding	2,350 s.f.
Roof Sheathing		2,310 s.f.	Asphalt Shingles	2,310 s.f.
Sub Flooring		630 s.f.	½'' Gypsum Drywall	5,806 s.f.
3½'' Wall Insulation		1,765 s.f.	Ceramic Tile	215 s.f.
6'' Ceiling Insulation		1,285 s.f.	Vinyl Tile	360 s.f.
1'' x 24'' Slab Insulation		132 l.f.	Carpet	114 s.y.
Windows (sliding)		9		

THE ASPEN

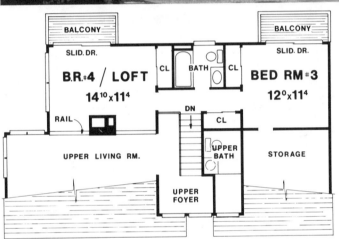

SECOND FLOOR PLAN

BALCONY

SLID. DR.

B.R.#4 / LOFT
14¹⁰x11⁴

RAIL

CL   BATH   CL

UPPER LIVING RM.

DN

CL

UPPER BATH

BALCONY

SLID. DR.

BED RM #3
12⁰x11⁴

STORAGE

UPPER FOYER

A modern vacation home combining a one story front with a two story rear. Clerestory windows have been inserted where the front and rear roofs meet, creating a distinctive and exciting exterior. Inside, the living room features a soaring sloped ceiling, windows and sliding glass doors on three sides, and a three-way brick fireplace. A kitchen barbecue adjoins the rear of the fireplace. Adjacent to the kitchen is a combination mud room, extra shower and dressing area, with access from the wraparound rear deck. The master bedroom with a full bath, and a smaller bedroom or den completes the first level. The second level contains a bedroom with an outside balcony, a full bath, a loft area overlooking the living room and a large storage area. Although shown on a basement for a sloping lot, blueprints also include provisions for building without the basement.

AREA DATA	First Floor	1,096 s.f.
	Second Floor	464 s.f.
	Opt. Basement	1,096 s.f.

MATERIAL LIST

Concrete	(s)	55.7 c.y.
	(b)	57.4 c.y.
Flitch Plates		2
Framing Lumber	(s)	11,390 b.f.
	(b)	14,484 b.f.
Wall Sheathing		1,800 s.f.
Roof Sheathing		1,400 s.f.
Sub Flooring		1,731 s.f.
3½'' Wall Insulation		1,400 s.f.
6'' Ceiling Insulation		1,230 s.f.
Windows (sliding)		9
(fixed)		13
Doors (exterior)		2
(ext. sliding)		9
(interior swing)		11
(int. closet)		7
Texture 1-11		1,800 s.f.
Asphalt Shingles		1,400 s.f.
½'' Gypsum Drywall		5,850 s.f.
Ceramic Tile		275 s.f.
Vinyl Tile		142 s.f.
Carpet		116 s.y.

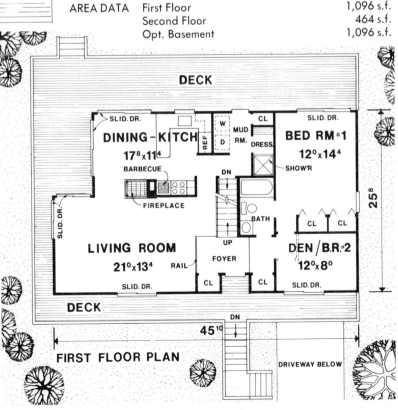

DECK

SLID. DR.

DINING - KITCH
17⁸x11⁴

REF

W D

MUD RM.

DRESS

CL

SLID. DR.

BED RM #1
12⁰x14⁴

BARBECUE

FIREPLACE

SLID. DR.

SHOW'R

DN

BATH

UP

LIVING ROOM
21⁰x13⁴

RAIL

FOYER

CL

CL

DEN / B.R.#2
12⁰x8⁰

CL   CL

SLID. DR.

DECK

SLID. DR.

25⁸

45¹⁰

DN

DRIVEWAY BELOW

FIRST FLOOR PLAN

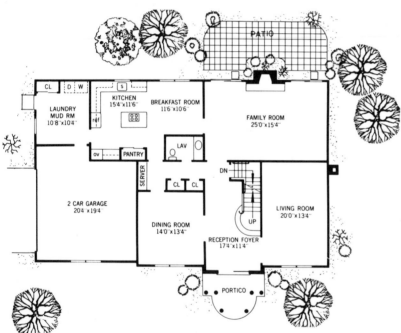

THE CARTIER

An elegant, traditional, two story, center halled home, with a columned front portico leading to a gracious reception foyer. Dual closets and a powder room are provided in the ante foyer. The living and dining rooms flank the reception foyer. The family room features a brick fireplace, beamed ceiling and two sets of sliding glass doors. The kitchen includes a pantry, center island cooking center and serving buffet to the dining room. A spacious breakfast room, laundry-mud room and two car garage round out the first floor. The second floor provides five bedrooms and two luxurious baths. The fifth bedroom could also serve as a sitting room off the master bedroom.

AREA DATA	First Floor	1,740 s.f.
	Second Floor	1,440 s.f.
	Part Basement	300 s.f.
	Opt. Full Basement	1,143 s.f.
	Overall Dimensions	60' x 36'

MATERIAL LIST

Concrete	(s)	75 c.y.	Doors (exterior)	2
	(b)	90 c.y.	(ext. sliding)	3
Brick Veneer		165 s.f.	(interior swing)	17
Framing Lumber	(s)	15,396 b.f.	(int. closet)	6
	(b)	17,695 b.f.	Wood Shingles	2,040 s.f.
Wall Sheathing		2,220 s.f.	Asphalt Shingles	2,660 s.f.
Roof Sheathing		2,660 s.f.	½'' Gypsum Drywall	10,120 s.f.
Sub Flooring		17,000 s.f.	Ceramic Tile	280 s.f.
3½'' Wall Insulation		2,350 s.f.	Vinyl Tile	446 s.f.
6'' Ceiling Insulation		1,750 s.f.	Oak Flooring	1,155 s.f.
1'' x 24'' Slab Insulation		114 l.f.	Carpet	120 s.y.
Windows (double hung)		17		

Making Changes

Making changes in stock plans is so common that it is likely that no two homes built from the same stock plans will be the same. Some of the usual reasons for making changes include personal taste, a particular lot condition or to suit local ordinances. Specifications regarding windows or other materials are often changed, and certain rooms enlarged and others reduced. Many other minor changes are often made during construction.

If the contemplated change is relatively simple, it can be resolved by making the appropriate "red-line" notation on the blueprints (or specification) to be used by the contractor. Even dimensional changes can be handled this way. If the change being considered is complicated, or involves major design or structural consideration, local professional help should be sought.

If an architect is available, he may be able to help. Expect charges to vary between $30 and $50 per hour on a consultation basis, to several hundred dollars to provide some revised sketch drawings. This will be money well spent to avoid costly errors, both aesthetic and functional. Remember, your total cost for plans will still be only a small fraction of the total cost of a personally designed home, as well as an insignificant part of the total house cost.

If professional help is not available, you can often rely on your builder, whose years of experience and intuitive knowledge should be of value. Most builders have worked from stock plans before and are familiar enough with the process of making changes. As a guide, the following common types of changes are frequently considered—and undertaken—by purchasers of stock plans.

1. Enlarging the home, lengthwise or in depth.
2. Removing or relocating interior partitions.
3. Adding brick (or stone) veneer.
4. Changing windows.
5. Changing exterior materials.
6. Basement vs. slab.
7. Relationship of garage floor to house floor.
8. Exterior fascia and trim details.
9. Cathedral ceilings.
10. Interior details, kitchen cabinets, fireplaces, etc.
11. Modifying the general specifications.
12. Adding or relocating a garage.
13. Changing floor heights (sinking a room).
14. Changes due to warm-air heating.
15. Changes to save energy.

Since detailed information on how to accomplish these changes is provided with the construction blueprints, you should not allow your desire to personalize or change things dissuade you from building from a published, pre-designed plan.

THE ADAMS

AREA DATA
First Floor   1,163 s.f.
Second Floor   771 s.f.
Opt. Basement   910 s.f.

A lovely, gambrel roofed, two story home, modest in size and practical to build. A rustic exterior and authentic details provide this home with an abundance of charm, yet its interior is as up to date as can be. Off the foyer and center hall, a sumptuous living room occupies the entire right section of the first floor; it includes a built-in wet bar and a fireplace. The eat-in kitchen is visually open to the adjacent family room, which offers the option of a second fireplace, sliding glass doors to the rear patio, and a second front entry, if desired. The second floor provides three bedrooms and two full baths.

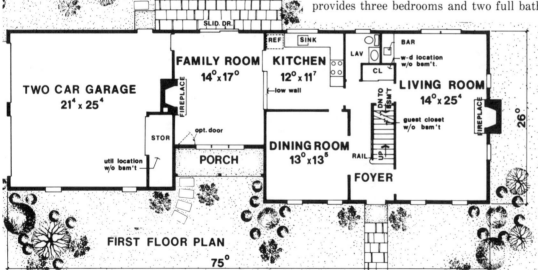

FIRST FLOOR PLAN

MATERIAL LIST

Concrete	(s)	52 c.y.	Doors (exterior)	2
	(b)	70 c.f.	(ext. sliding)	1
Framing Lumber	(s)	9,670 b.f.	(interior swing)	14
	(b)	11,632 b.f.	(int. closet)	5
Wall Sheathing		2,020 s.f.	Board & Batten Siding	2,020 s.f.
Roof Sheathing		2,310 s.f.	Asphalt Shingles	2,310 s.f.
Sub Flooring		1,640 s.f.	½'' Gypsum Drywall	6,230 s.f.
3½'' Wall Insulation		1,860 s.f.	Ceramic Tile	230 s.f.
6'' Ceiling Insulation		2,400 s.f.	Vinyl Tile	140 s.f.
1'' x 24'' Slab Insulation		132 l.f.	Carpet	165 s.y.
Windows (double hung)		23		

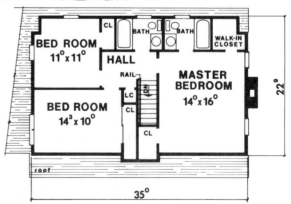

SECOND FLOOR PLAN

THIS IS A COVER HOUSE

THE DORCHESTER

A center hall, two story colonial that suggests luxury throughout. Elegance at an affordable price permeates the design. The one major indulgence is the circular staircase that highlights the foyer. The balance of the first floor is a classic layout, dining room to one side, living room to the other, and daily living areas to the rear. The family room features a full wall fireplace with a log bin, and sliding doors to the rear. The second floor provides four bedrooms, two luxurious baths, plus a sumptuous master dressing area. An oversized two car garage is included with the house. Blueprints include plans for an optional full basement.

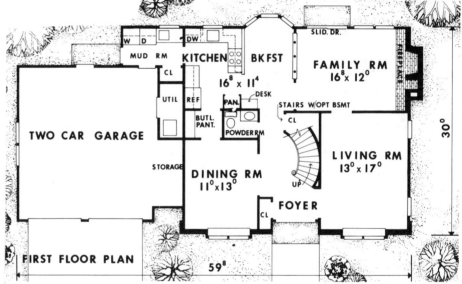

FIRST FLOOR PLAN

AREA DATA	First Floor	1,039 s.f.
	Second Floor	1,040 s.f.
	Opt. Basement	1,040 s.f.

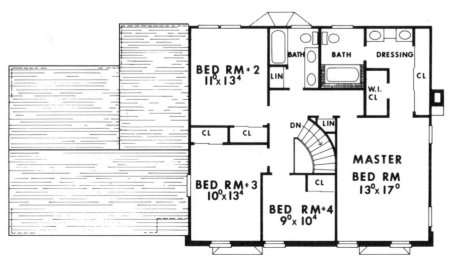

SECOND FLOOR PLAN

MATERIAL LIST

Concrete	(s)	49 c.y.
	(b)	65 c.y.
Brick Veneer		310 s.f.
Framing Lumber	(s)	10,436 b.f.
	(b)	12,877 b.f.
Wall Sheathing		2,400 s.f.
Roof Sheathing		2,050 s.f.
Sub Flooring		1,010 s.f.
3½″ Wall Insulation		1,820 s.f.
6″ Ceiling Insulation		1,100 s.f.
1″ x 24″ Slab Insulation		128 l.f.
Windows (single hung)		26
Doors (exterior)		2
(ext. sliding)		1
(interior swing)		18
(int. closet)		5
Wood Shingles		1,600 s.f.
Exterior Plywood		200 s.f.
Asphalt Shingles		2,050 s.f.
½″ Gypsum Drywall		8,000 s.f.
Ceramic Tile		300 s.f.
Vinyl Tile		260 s.f.
Oak Flooring		806 s.f.
Carpet		80 s.y.

THE BEDFORD

AREA DATA Living Area   2,451 s.f.

Although the exterior style of this large, charming, rustic looking, three bedroom ranch is traditional, the interior is dramatically contemporary. The double door opens to a spacious, sloped ceiling foyer, which is separated from the sloped ceilinged, sunken living and dining rooms by a brick planter and rails. The living room features built-in bookcases on either side of the two-way brick fireplace that it shares with the adjacent family room. Built-in bookcases are also provided in the family room as is a cathedral ceiling and a sliding door to the patio. The adjacent breakfast room and kitchen, with their lovely front-to-rear view, are near the mud room, lavatory and two car garage. The bedroom wing includes a magnificent master suite with an enormous walk-in closet and a lavish compartmented bath.

MATERIAL LIST

Concrete	76 c.y.	Doors (exterior)	3
Brick Veneer	260 s.f.	(ext. sliding)	2
Framing Lumber	11,774 b.f.	(interior swing)	11
Wall Sheathing	1,980 s.f.	(int. closet)	6
Roof Sheathing	3,700 s.f.	Exterior Siding	1,600 s.f.
3½'' Wall Insulation	1,550 s.f.	Asphalt Shingles	3,700 s.f.
6'' Ceiling Insulation	2,780 s.f.	½'' Gypsum Drywall	6,860 s.f.
1'' x 24'' Slab Insulation	200 l.f.	Ceramic Tile	325 s.f.
Windows (double hung)	12	Vinyl Tile	300 s.f.
(fixed)	1	Carpet	185 s.y.
(casement)	4		

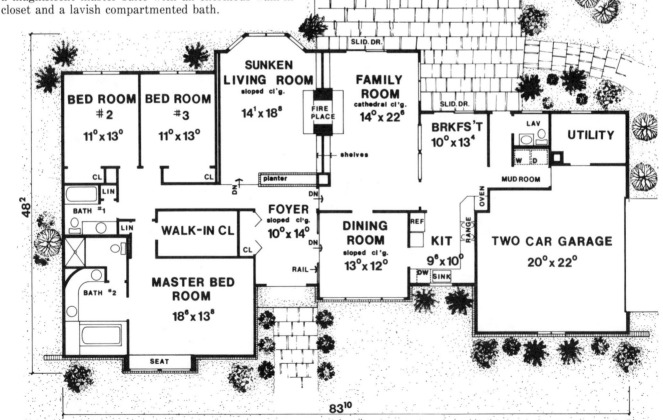

FLOOR PLAN

THE NORMANDIE

A French mansion resplendent in exterior appeal and sumptuous in its plan. Double doors lead to a magnificent reception foyer and center hall, highlighted by a sweeping circular style staircase. A banquet-sized dining room is to the left and a spacious living room to the right; both have projecting front bay windows. A breakfast room adjoins the fantastic kitchen. The sunken family room has nine-foot ceilings, a brick fireplace with log bin and sliding glass doors to the rear patio. The laundry-mud room area includes a full bath, rear entrance and a maid's or sewing room. Two of the three second floor hall bedrooms are master size. The luxurious master suite includes a spacious bedroom, two walk-in closets, a boudoir and a sumptuous private bath with sunken tub and sloped ceiling. Bonus space over the garage is large enough for a full apartment or four more bedrooms, or just storage space.

AREA DATA	First Floor	2,107 s.f.
	Second Floor	1,795 s.f.
	Basement	1,795 s.f.

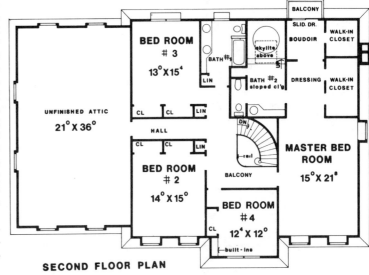

SECOND FLOOR PLAN

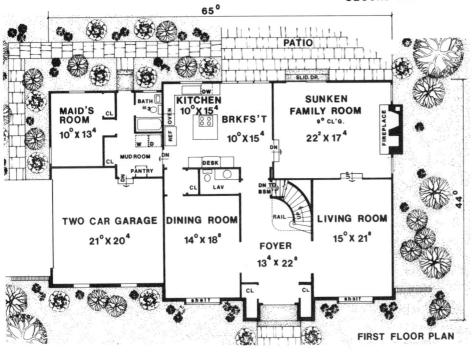

FIRST FLOOR PLAN

MATERIAL LIST

Concrete	113 c.y.
Brick Veneer	554 s.f.
Flitch Plates	1
Framing Lumber	24,672 b.f.
Wall Sheathing	1,350 s.f.
Roof Sheathing	4,880 s.f.
Sub Flooring	3,520 s.f.
3½'' Wall Insulation	2,600 s.f.
6'' Ceiling Insulation	2,920 s.f.
1'' x 24'' Slab Insulation	58 l.f.
Windows (single hung)	23
(oriole)	9
Doors (exterior)	3
(ext. sliding)	2
(interior swing)	21
(int. closet)	8
Texture 1-11 Siding	890 s.f.
Asphalt Shingles	4,880 s.f.
½'' Gypsum Drywall	11,430 s.f.
Ceramic Tile	402 s.f.
Vinyl Tile	570 s.f.
Carpet	285 s.y.

THE ELMWOOD

MATERIAL LIST

Concrete	(s)	61 c.y.	Doors (exterior)		2
	(b)	90 c.y.	(ext. sliding)		2
Flitch Plates		1	(interior swing)		8
Framing Lumber	(s)	8,010 b.f.	(int. closet)		5
	(b)	11,250 b.f.	Wood Shingles		1,556 s.f.
Wall Sheathing		1,440 s.f.	Asphalt Shingles		2,640 s.f.
Roof Sheathing		2,640 s.f.	½'' Gypsum Drywall		6,700 s.f.
3½'' Wall Insulation		1,263 s.f.	Ceramic Tile		208 s.f.
6'' Ceiling Insulation		1,490 s.f.	Vinyl Tile		172 s.f.
1'' x 24'' Slab Insulation		152 l.f.	Carpet		139 s.y.
Windows (double hung)		14			

With its angled garage and large colonial windows, this rambling ranch appears larger than its modest square footage indicates. A well organized and simple plan also gives this house a spacious and open feeling. The living room (276 sq. ft.) is adjacent to the dining room which includes glass doors to a covered rear porch. The family room, with its fireplace and cathedral ceiling, also opens to the porch. The bedroom wing consists of three bedrooms, a hall bath, plus a half bath and two walk-in closets in the master bedroom.

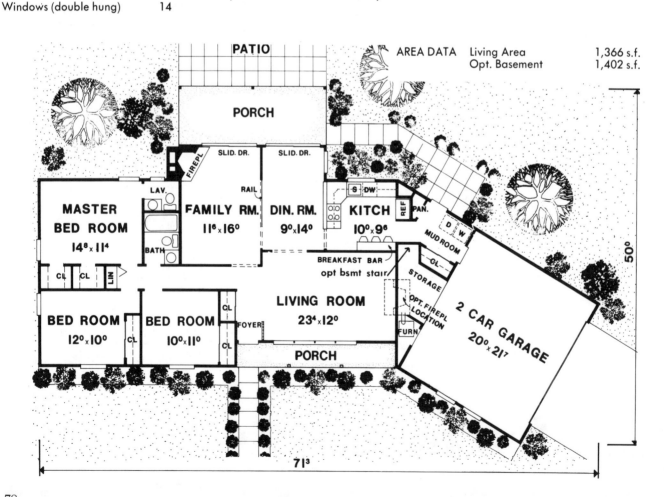

AREA DATA	Living Area	1,366 s.f.
	Opt. Basement	1,402 s.f.

THE BURGUNDY

An appealing, French provincial styled, four bedroom split-level home. The L-shaped living-dining room features sliding glass doors to a rear patio. The breakfast area of the efficient kitchen has a large double window providing an expansive view of the rear. Four bedrooms and two full baths are provided on the bedroom level, with the master bedroom including a dressing area with vanity and sink and a sliding glass door to a rear balcony. The lower level contains a garage, lavatory, convenient mud room, side entry and a family room with a brick fireplace occupying an entire side wall. The breakfast area has a rail overlooking the family room, and there are sliding doors from the family room to the rear.

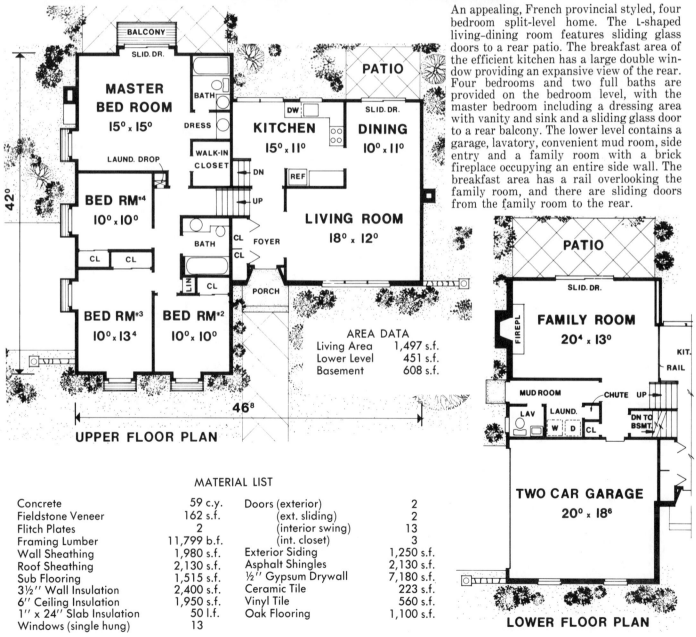

AREA DATA

Living Area 1,497 s.f.
Lower Level 451 s.f.
Basement 608 s.f.

UPPER FLOOR PLAN

LOWER FLOOR PLAN

MATERIAL LIST

Concrete	59 c.y.	Doors (exterior)	2
Fieldstone Veneer	162 s.f.	(ext. sliding)	2
Flitch Plates	2	(interior swing)	13
Framing Lumber	11,799 b.f.	(int. closet)	3
Wall Sheathing	1,980 s.f.	Exterior Siding	1,250 s.f.
Roof Sheathing	2,130 s.f.	Asphalt Shingles	2,130 s.f.
Sub Flooring	1,515 s.f.	½'' Gypsum Drywall	7,180 s.f.
3½'' Wall Insulation	2,400 s.f.	Ceramic Tile	223 s.f.
6'' Ceiling Insulation	1,950 s.f.	Vinyl Tile	560 s.f.
1'' x 24'' Slab Insulation	50 l.f.	Oak Flooring	1,100 s.f.
Windows (single hung)	13		

THE CHATHAM

A delightfully charming, L-shaped, traditional ranch of gracious proportions; it orients most rooms to the rear. The dynamic kitchen of this informal, country-style home includes a desk, pantry and bay windowed breakfast area. A laundry-mud room off the kitchen provides access to the two car garage and side yard. The family room features a full brick wall fireplace and sliding glass doors to the rear. The sunken living room includes a large bay window, and is separated from the center hall by a rail, affording a view from the entrance foyer and adjacent dining room through to the rear. The master bedroom features a dressing area, walk-in closet and private bath.

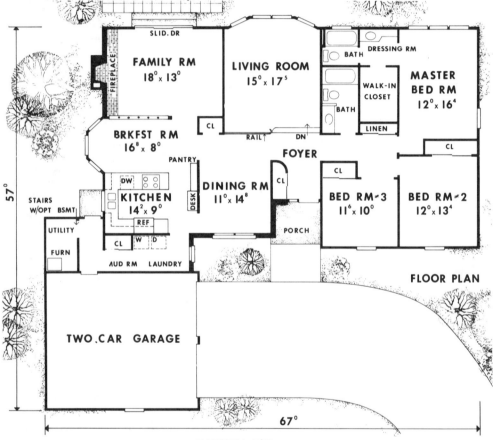

FLOOR PLAN

AREA DATA

Living Area	2,003 s.f.
Opt. Basement	2,039 s.f.

MATERIAL LIST

Concrete	(s)	65 c.y.	Doors (exterior)		3
	(b)	90 c.y.	(ext. sliding)		1
Masonry Veneer		155 s.f.	(interior swing)		8
Framing Lumber	(s)	9,231 b.f.	(int. closet)		5
	(b)	13,692 b.f.	Exterior Siding		1,780 s.f.
Wall Sheathing		2,500 s.f.	Asphalt Shingles		3,080 s.f.
Roof Sheathing		3,080 s.f.	½'' Gypsum Drywall		5,900 s.f.
3½'' Wall Insulation		1,350 s.f.	Ceramic Tile		210 s.f.
6'' Ceiling Insulation		2,000 s.f.	Vinyl Tile		360 s.f.
1'' x 24'' Slab Insulation		180 l.f.	Oak Flooring		1,360 s.f.
Windows (double hung)		15			
(dbl. dome skylight)		1			
(bsmt. sash)		5			

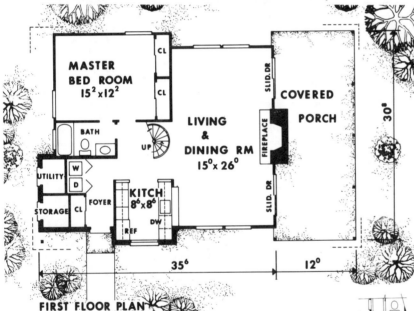

FIRST FLOOR PLAN

MASTER BED ROOM 15²x12²
LIVING & DINING RM 15⁰x 26⁰
COVERED PORCH
BATH
UTILITY
STORAGE
FOYER
KITCH 8⁶x 8⁶
FIREPLACE
SLID. DR
30⁸
35⁶
12⁰

THE WOODLAKE

The exterior appeal of this charming vacation home stems from its rustic, log cabin appearance. Inside, there is an efficient kitchen to the right of the entrance foyer and a utility-laundry area to the left. The living-dining room features a soaring sloped ceiling, a rustic stone fireplace and sliding doors to a large covered porch. The master bedroom and a full bath complete the first floor. Two second floor bedrooms and a bath are reached via a beautiful circular staircase. A skylight overhead provides extra brightness. Working drawings include a slab foundation or an optional full basement.

AREA DATA | First Floor | 928 s.f.
| Second Floor | 375 s.f.
| Opt. Basement | 928 s.f.

PART PLAN W/OPT BSMT

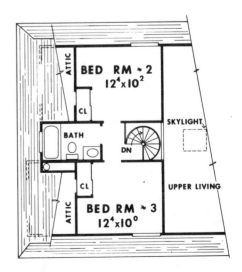

SECOND FLOOR PLAN

BED RM 2 12⁴x10²
BED RM 3 12⁴x10⁰
ATTIC
SKYLIGHT
UPPER LIVING
BATH

MATERIAL LIST

Concrete	(s)	38 c.y.	Doors (exterior)	3
	(b)	56 c.y.	(ext. sliding)	2
Stone Veneer		230 s.f.	(interior swing)	6
Framing Lumber	(s)	7,148 b.f.	(int. closet)	5
	(b)	9,368 b.f.	Log Cabin Siding	1,144 s.f.
Wall Sheathing		1,280 s.f.	Asphalt Shingles	1,990 s.f.
Roof Sheathing		1,990 s.f.	½'' Gypsum Drywall	4,460 s.f.
Sub Flooring		440 s.f.	Ceramic Tile	200 s.f.
3½'' Wall Insulation		1,370 s.f.	Vinyl Tile	86 s.f.
6'' Ceiling Insulation		844 s.f.	Oak Flooring	268 s.f.
1'' x 24'' Slab Insulation		126 l.f.	Carpet	82 s.y.
Windows (casement)		9		
(awning)		2		

28⁰	17⁴
BASIC 2ND FLOOR	OPT. MASTER B.R. SUITE

MASTER BED ROOM
16⁰ x 11⁶

BATH

OPT. BATH

DRS'G

OPT. WLK-IN CLOS

WLK-IN CLOS.

DN

RAIL

OPT. BED RM.#4
17⁰ x 13⁰

BED RM.#2
10⁰ x 13²

LIN

CL

BED RM.#3
11⁶ x 9⁸

W.I. CL.

ROOF

SECOND FLOOR PLAN

THE KENSINGTON

Another popular, colonial styled, two story home—attractive to look at and practical to live in. A formal center hall entry leads to all parts, including the step down living and dining rooms at either side. Both the kitchen and dinette face the rear patio. The adjacent family room features a brick fireplace and sliding glass doors. The laundry-mud room area provides a powder room and access to the garage and rear yard. The second floor provides three bedrooms, a dual entry bath, plus space for a master suite and second full bath, to be finished initially or left for later. A two car garage is included, and an optional basement is available.

AREA DATA	First Floor	1,004 s.f.
	Second Floor	719 s.f.
	Opt. 4th Bedroom	344 s.f.
	Opt. Basement	1,004 s.f.

MATERIAL LIST

Concrete	(s)	42 c.y.
	(b)	63 c.y.
Brick Veneer		60 s.f.
Framing Lumber	(s)	7,411 b.f.
	(b)	9,446 b.f.
Wall Sheathing		2,285 s.f.
Roof Sheathing		1,660 s.f.
Sub Flooring		695 s.f.
3½'' Wall Insulation		1,850 s.f.
6'' Ceiling Insulation		1,170 s.f.
1'' x 24'' Slab Insulation		112 l.f.
Windows (single hung)		19
Doors (exterior)		2
(ext. sliding)		1
(interior swing)		15
(int. closet)		2
Wood Shingles		1,895 s.f.
Texture 1-11		136 s.f.
Asphalt Shingles		1,660 s.f.
½'' Gypsum Drywall		6,330 s.f.
Ceramic Tile		264 s.f.
Vinyl Tile		225 s.f.
Oak Flooring		1,150 s.f.
Slate		46 s.f.
Carpet		127 s.y.

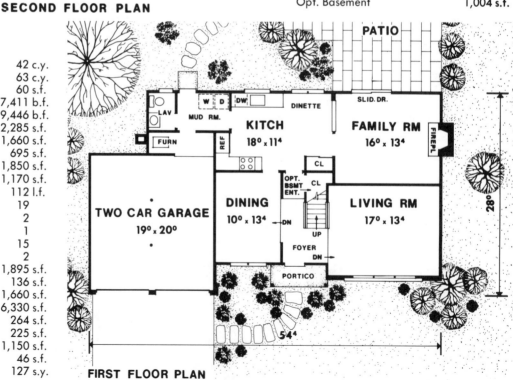

PATIO

W D DW SLID. DR.

LAV

MUD RM.

KITCH
18⁰ x 11⁴

DINETTE

FAMILY RM
16⁰ x 13⁴

FIREPL

FURN

REF

CL

OPT. BSMT ENT.

CL

TWO CAR GARAGE
19⁰ x 20⁰

DINING
10⁰ x 13⁴

DN

UP

FOYER

DN

LIVING RM
17⁰ x 13⁴

28⁰

PORTICO

54⁴

FIRST FLOOR PLAN

THE GREENWICH

Through the brick entrance, an enclosed atrium garden beckons one to enter a most unusual, contemporary, H-shaped, four bedroom ranch. Straight ahead from the entrance foyer lies an angular, expansive living room that features a dramatic cathedral ceiling and a rear window wall that includes sliding glass doors that lead to the enclosed rear patio. This lovely patio is also accessible from the family room and the master bedroom. To the left of the foyer, Spanish arches lead to the in-line dining room, kitchen, family room wing. The efficient, well equipped kitchen includes a built-in breakfast bar that adjoins the family room. To the right of the foyer, a separate center hall connects the four bedrooms with the foyer and living room.

MATERIAL LIST

Concrete	102 c.y.
Brick Veneer	326 s.f.
Framing Lumber	7,511 b.f.
Wall Sheathing	2,215 s.f.
Roof Sheathing	2,435 s.f.
3½" Wall Insulation	1,700 s.f.
6" Ceiling Insulation	1,740 s.f.
1" x 24" Slab Insulation	276 l.f.
Windows (alum. sgl. hung)	10
(fixed)	2
Doors (exterior)	2
(ext. sliding)	4
(interior swing)	12
(int. closet)	4
Texture 1-11	1,850 s.f.
Asphalt Shingles	2,450 s.f.
½" Gypsum Drywall	6,784 s.f.
Ceramic Tile	140 s.f.
Vinyl Tile	326 s.f.
Carpet	132 s.y.
Slate Floor	55 s.f.

AREA DATA

Living Area	1,785 s.f.
Overall Dimensions	44' x 56'

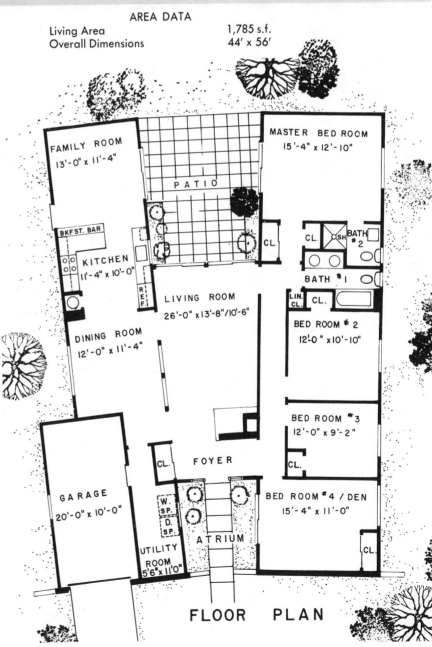

FLOOR PLAN

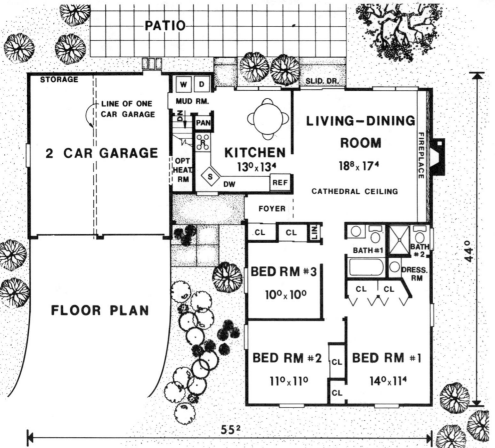

FLOOR PLAN

PATIO

STORAGE

LINE OF ONE CAR GARAGE

2 CAR GARAGE

W | D

MUD RM.

SLID. DR.

PAN

LIVING–DINING ROOM
18^8 x 17^4

KITCHEN
13^0 x 13^4

OPT HEAT RM

S

DW | REF

FIREPLACE

CATHEDRAL CEILING

FOYER

CL | CL | LIN

BED RM #3
10^0 x 10^0

BATH #1 | BATH #2

DRESS. RM

CL | CL

BED RM #2
11^0 x 11^0

CL | CL

BED RM #1
14^0 x 11^4

44^0

55^2

THE LAUREL

AREA DATA

Living Area	1,232 s.f.
Opt. Half Basement	625 s.f.
Opt. Basement	1,232 s.f.

The most distinctive and dramatic feature of this classic, L-shaped, traditional ranch is the unusually beautiful combination living-dining room. It features sliding glass doors to the patio, an impressive fireplace with wall to wall brick and a cathedral ceiling. The adjacent eat-in kitchen provides abundant cabinet space in an L-shape. The bedroom wing consists of three bedrooms with ample closet space and a separate dressing room in the master bedroom. The home should prove economical to construct, whether in its slab, half-basement or full basement versions.

MATERIAL LIST

Concrete	(s)	60 c.y.	Doors (exterior)	3
	(b)	63 c.y.	(ext. sliding)	1
Framing Lumber	(s)	7,715 b.f.	(interior swing)	10
	(b)	8,509 b.f.	(int. closet)	5
Wall Sheathing		1,840 s.f.	Wood Shingles	1,500 s.f.
Roof Sheathing		2,150 s.f.	Asphalt Shingles	2,100 s.f.
Sub Flooring		580 s.f.	½'' Gypsum Drywall	5,510 s.f.
3½'' Wall Insulation		1,780 s.f.	Ceramic Tile	146 s.f.
6'' Ceiling Insulation		890 s.f.	Vinyl Tile	160 s.f.
1'' x 24'' Slab Insulation		75 l.f.	Oak Flooring	325 s.f.
Windows (double hung)		10	Carpet	55 s.y.

Contracting the Building

After you obtain construction blueprints you can begin to get your home built. If you intend to make substantial changes, these should be resolved prior to doing anything. If the changes are minor, you can wait to finalize these with the contractor who will eventually build your home.

The plans (and specifications) should be given to several contractors to obtain firm proposals as to cost. If you intend to act as your own general contractor, distribute the plans to the various subcontractors and suppliers to obtain firm quotes. Always, whenever possible, obtain two or more proposals. This is suggested not only as a check on prices, but also to obtain additional comments and suggestions, as well as offer some security that there was no major oversight on the part of the contractor which could cause difficulties later.

You should resolve with your contractor all choices of materials, particularly where the level of quality is important. Also, finalize the so-called options or extras (fireplaces, floor finishes, cabinets, appliances, light fixtures, air conditioning, storm windows, gutters and leaders, site improvements such as driveway, walks, patios and landscaping, etc.) and have these noted on the plans and specifications, as necessary. You should also discuss a time schedule.

On Choosing a Contractor

It should be stated at the outset that most custom home contractors are reliable, honest individuals, and the very few who are not have created an image well beyond their real numbers! To assure yourself that you do not become involved with one of the latter, here are a handful of very simple rules to follow:

1. Always obtain more than one estimate.
2. Never choose a contractor based solely on lowest price.
3. Don't rely on possible legal remedies as your protection against someone you are apprehensive about to begin with. Simply, don't hire him.
4. Don't hire the contractor who only suggests changes that will reduce the price (and possibly the quality). Also, don't hire the opposite, one who only suggests more expensive changes. There should be a balance.
5. Choose a contractor based heavily on past performance. Ask him for the names of people he has built for in the past. Call them, and visit them if possible.
6. Choose a contractor based on recommendations of local businessmen he deals with (bankers, material suppliers, local officials).
7. Choose a contractor who appears knowledgeable and whose overall attitude is helpful—one who appears to have your interest at heart.

The Do-It-Yourself Contractor

A final word to those who are considering acting as their own general contractor. If you have not built a home before, have little or no knowledge of construction and your main motivation for acting as your own contractor is to save cost, think twice about it. You will have to put in a great deal of time and effort to accomplish the building. If you value your time, you may find yourself spending more timewise than you will have saved by not hiring a general contractor—even if everything goes right and problems are at a minimum.

If, by necessity or choice, you feel you must be your own contractor and you are apprehensive, seek all the help you can. Sometimes a key subcontractor, such as a carpenter, can help you coordinate the construction activities and help put "things" into place. If you are somewhat knowledgeable and looking forward to the prospect of building your own home, you should find it to be one of the most rewarding experiences of your life.

In any case, if you are building a home, read all you can on the subject. This general overview pinpoints likely places for error, but it is far from all-inclusive. Further reading is strongly suggested.

THE SOMERSET

A charming, comfortably sized, three bedroom ranch with a distinctive three tiered foor, arched portico and large, colonial windows. A central foyer leads to the three basic areas of the home, with the formal living room and dining room occupying front center. The informal, rear facing, cathedral ceilinged family room includes a brick fireplace: the eat-in kitchen with its pantry closet, cathedral ceiling and sliding doors to the patio adjoins the family room. Adjacent to the kitchen, the mud room provides access to the yard, basement, and side entry, two car garage. The bedroom wing includes three nice-sized bedrooms, ample closets and two full baths. Blueprints include slab on grade and full basement versions.

MATERIAL LIST

Concrete	(s)	60 c.y.	Doors (exterior)		2
	(b)	86 c.y.	(ext. sliding)		1
Brick Veneer		80 s.f.	(interior swing)		9
Framing Lumber	(s)	9,409 b.f.	(int. closet)		5
	(b)	13,162 b.f.	Wood Shingles		1,580 s.f.
Wall Sheathing		1,680 s.f.	Asphalt Shingles		3,000 s.f.
Roof Sheathing		3,000 s.f.	½″ Gypsum Drywall		5,585 s.f.
3½″ Wall Insulation		1,742 s.f.	Ceramic Tile		121 s.f.
6″ Ceiling Insulation		1,825 s.f.	Vinyl Tile		265 s.f.
1″ x 24″ Slab Insulation		193 l.f.	Carpet		148 s.y.
Windows (double hung)		15			
(fixed)		1			

AREA DATA

Living Area	1,907 s.f.
Opt. Basement	1,750 s.f.

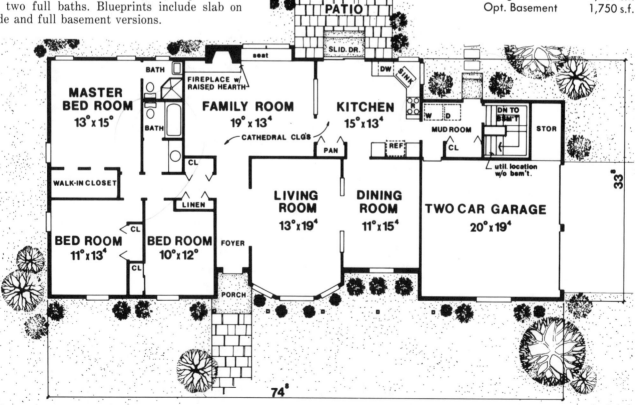

FIRST FLOOR PLAN

THE CYPRESS

A contemporary styled vacation home, designed to permit you to personalize it to fit your lot—and budget. The living-dining room features a magnificent window wall, brick fireplace and a soaring two-story-high cathedral ceiling. Two nice-sized bedrooms, a full bath, convenient laundry alcove and efficient kitchen complete the first floor. Two more bedrooms and a full bath occupy the second floor. An optional oversized garage together with a screened porch creates an attractive single story contrast to the main structure. Other options include a large rear deck, barbecue behind the fireplace and a choice of a full basement or slab on grade construction.

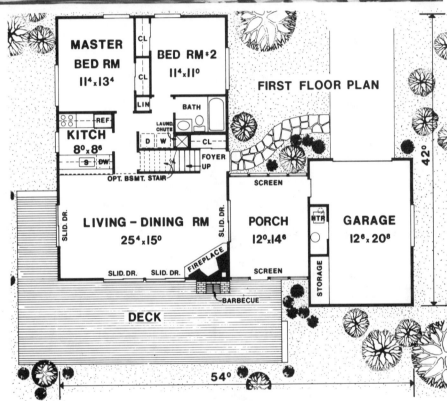

FIRST FLOOR PLAN

MASTER BED RM 11⁴×13⁴
BED RM #2 11⁴×11⁰
KITCH 8⁰×8⁶
BATH
LIVING – DINING RM 25⁴×15⁰
PORCH 12⁰×14⁶
GARAGE 12⁶×20⁸
DECK
FIREPLACE
BARBECUE
STORAGE
SCREEN
OPT. BSMT. STAIR
FOYER UP
42⁰
54⁰

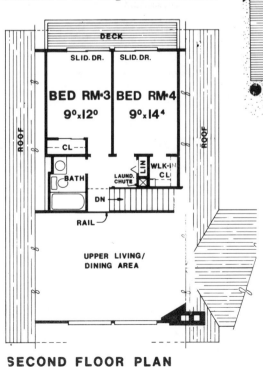

SECOND FLOOR PLAN

DECK
SLID. DR.   SLID. DR.
BED RM #3 9⁰×12⁰
BED RM #4 9⁰×14⁴
CL
BATH
WLK-IN CL
LAUND. CHUTE   LIN
DN
RAIL
UPPER LIVING/DINING AREA
ROOF

AREA DATA

First Floor	988 s.f.	
Second Floor	400 s.f.	
Opt. Basement	988 s.f.	

MATERIAL LIST

Concrete	(s)	15 c.y.	Doors (exterior)	1
	(b)	26 c.y.	(ext. sliding)	5
Framing Lumber	(s)	9,729 b.f.	(interior swing)	9
	(b)	11,681 b.f.	(int. closet)	4
Wall Sheathing		1,396 s.f.	Texture 1-11	1,300 s.f.
Roof Sheathing		2,200 s.f.	Asphalt Shingles	2,200 s.f.
Sub Flooring		4,000 s.f.	½'' Gypsum Drywall	5,940 s.f.
3½'' Wall Insulation		1,300 s.f.	Ceramic Tile	170 s.f.
6'' Ceiling Insulation		1,500 s.f.	Vinyl Tile	40 s.f.
1'' x 24'' Slab Insulation		130 l.f.	Oak Flooring	375 s.f.
Windows (sliding)		5	Carpet	90 s.y.
(fixed)		6		

THE GRANADA

AREA DATA
Living Area   2,674 s.f.
Basement   1,558 s.f.

A spacious, contemporary ranch with a woodsy, informal look. Inside, the center hall plan, however, provides greater formality. The dining room occupies front center, while the living room is toward the rear. A large U-shaped kitchen includes an attractive bayed rear dinette. The glamorous family room, at the far end of the home, is distinguished by a soaring cathedral ceiling, a large brick fireplace wall and access to the rear patio. The mud room includes ample laundry and freezer space, a walk-in pantry and access to the oversized two car garage. The bedroom wing provides four generous sized bedrooms and two full baths. The master suite includes a walk-in closet, dressing alcove and private bath. The home includes a part basement.

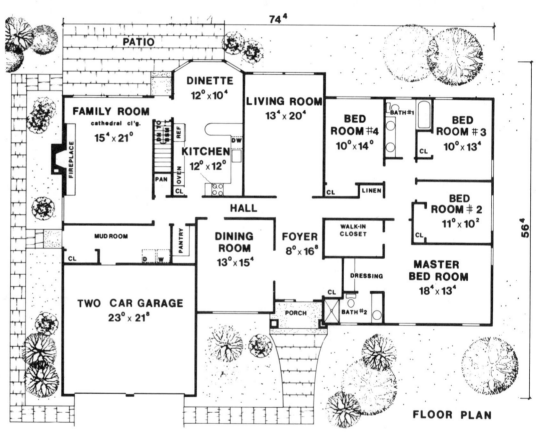

FLOOR PLAN

MATERIAL LIST

Concrete	85 c.y.	Doors (exterior)	3
Framing Lumber	14,690 b.f.	(interior swing)	12
Wall Sheathing	2,600 s.f.	(int. closet)	4
Roof Sheathing	3,890 s.f.	Texture 1-11	2,550 s.f.
Sub Flooring	1,470 s.f.	Asphalt Shingles	3,890 s.f.
3½'' Wall Insulation	2,090 s.f.	½'' Gypsum Drywall	8,960 s.f.
6'' Ceiling Insulation	2,750 s.f.	Ceramic Tile	222 s.f.
1'' x 24'' Slab Insulation	129 l.f.	Vinyl Tile	227 s.f.
Windows (alum. sgl. hung)	17	Oak Flooring	1,292 s.f.
(fixed)	4	Carpet	108 s.y.

THE MARQUETTE

An elegant, French provincial styled, two story home that is large enough to be comfortable, yet practical enough to become reality. The covered front portico leads to a spacious reception foyer, which in turn provides direct access to all rooms. The living room and dining room are both generous in size, yet not pompous. The family room features a fireplace with log bin, as well as sliding doors to the rear. The lavish kitchen includes a center island with dual cooktops, and adjoins a spacious bay windowed breakfast room. The second floor provides four bedrooms and two bathrooms. The master bedroom includes a large walk-in closet, double basin vanity and bidet in the bath.

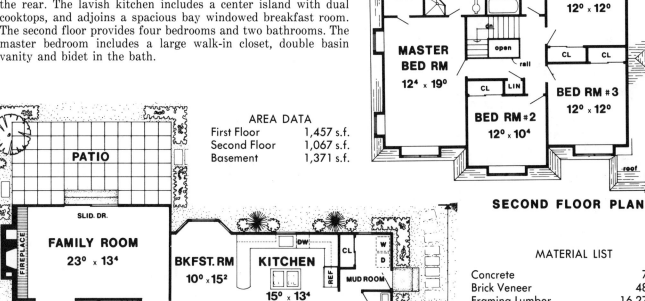

SECOND FLOOR PLAN

AREA DATA

First Floor	1,457 s.f.
Second Floor	1,067 s.f.
Basement	1,371 s.f.

FIRST FLOOR PLAN

MATERIAL LIST

Concrete	79 c.y.
Brick Veneer	480 s.f.
Framing Lumber	16,271 b.f.
Wall Sheathing	1,360 s.f.
Roof Sheathing	2,950 s.f.
Sub Flooring	2,500 s.f.
3½″ Wall Insulation	2,322 s.f.
6″ Ceiling Insulation	1,550 s.f.
Windows (single hung)	20
(oriole)	4
Doors (exterior)	3
(ext. sliding)	1
(interior swing)	13
(int. closet)	4
Exterior Siding	775 s.f.
Asphalt Shingles	2,950 s.f.
½″ Gypsum Drywall	8,530 s.f.
Ceramic Tile	250 s.f.
Vinyl Tile	420 s.f.
Oak Flooring	1,710 s.f.

THE JUNIPER

AREA DATA   Living Area   1,289 s.f.
           Mud Room, Utility   96 s.f.
           Opt. Basement   1,385 s.f.

An attractive looking modest size, three bedroom contemporary ranch with center hall. A sheltered porch leads to a modest foyer and to the center hall. Adjacent to the foyer is a cathedral ceilinged living room with wraparound corner windows and a large brick fireplace. The spacious country kitchen provides ample area for eating, and includes a sliding glass door to the rear patio. The adjoining laundry-mud room includes a pantry and entrance to the garage. Three bedrooms, two full baths and a formal dining room complete the home. Options include a one or two car garage, full basement, and a garden room behind the two car garage, all of which are included in construction blueprints.

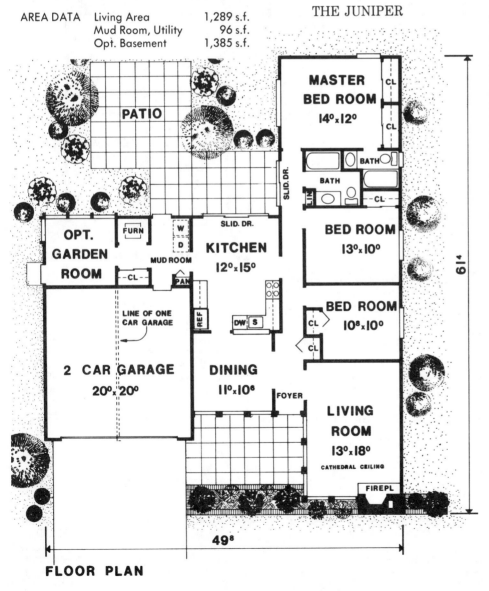

FLOOR PLAN

MATERIAL LIST

Concrete	(s)	57 c.y.
	(b)	82 c.y.
Flitch Plates		1
Framing Lumber	(s)	8,840 b.f.
	(b)	11,608 b.f.
Wall Sheathing		1,600 s.f.
Roof Sheathing		2,528 s.f.
3½'' Wall Insulation		1,400 s.f.
6'' Ceiling Insulation		1,400 s.f.
1'' x 24'' Slab Insulation		200 l.f.
Windows (sliding)		18
(fixed)		3
Doors (exterior)		3
(ext. sliding)		1
(interior swing)		11
(int. closet)		7
Texture 1-11		1,600 s.f.
Asphalt Shingles		2,550 s.f.
½'' Gypsum Drywall		4,820 s.f.
Ceramic Tile		175 s.f.
Vinyl Tile		270 s.f.
Carpet		112 s.y.

THE PINEWOOD

AREA DATA	Ground Floor	579 s.f.
	Main Floor	777 s.f.
	Loft	201 s.f.
	Opt. Basement	471 s.f.

This dramatic vacation home features an exciting living and dining room which has windows on three sides, a soaring sloped ceiling and a stone fireplace. The lower level contains a slate entrance foyer, two bedrooms, bath, utility room, and garage. On the main level, situated high for scenic enhancement, are the living–dining room, unusual semi-circular kitchen and the master bedroom with spacious closets. The up staircase is also housed in a dramatic semi-circular shape. The upper loft space can be used for a variety of uses. An optional greenhouse on the main deck is included in the blueprints.

GROUND FLOOR PLAN

PATIO

UTILITY RM.

CL

W
D

CL

BED RM
10¹⁰ x 12⁰

BATH

BED RM
11⁰ x 13⁰

GARAGE
12¹⁰ x 20⁰

STORAGE

FOYER

SLID. DR.

UP

CL

PATIO

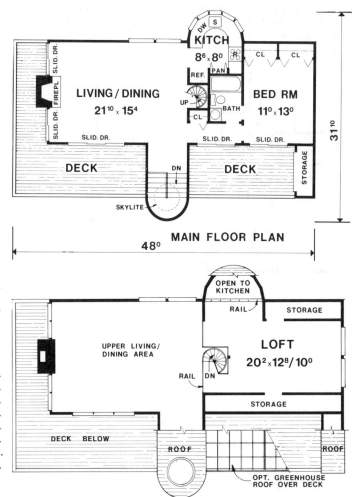

MAIN FLOOR PLAN — 48⁰ — 31¹⁰

KITCH
8⁶ x 8⁰

DW S

CL   CL

REF.   PAN

FIREPL

SLID. DR.

LIVING / DINING
21¹⁰ x 15⁴

UP

BATH

CL

BED RM
11⁰ x 13⁰

SLID. DR.

DECK

SLID. DR.

SLID. DR.

DECK

STORAGE

DN

SKYLITE

OPEN TO KITCHEN

RAIL

STORAGE

UPPER LIVING/ DINING AREA

LOFT
20² x 12⁸/10⁰

RAIL   DN

STORAGE

DECK BELOW

ROOF

ROOF

OPT. GREENHOUSE ROOF OVER DECK

MATERIAL LIST

Concrete	(s)	39 c.y.	(sliding)		9
	(b)	51 c.y.	(fixed)		124 s.f.
Stone Veneer		305 s.f.	Doors (exterior)		3
Flitch Plates		3	(ext. sliding)		6
Framing Lumber	(s)	9,224 b.f.	(interior swing)		12
	(b)	10,488 b.f.	(int. closet)		7
Wall Sheathing		2,340 s.f.	Exterior Siding		2,710 s.f.
Roof Sheathing		1,230 s.f.	Asphalt Shingles		1,230 s.f.
Sub Flooring		980 s.f.	½″ Gypsum Drywall		6,390 s.f.
3½″ Wall Insulation		1,965 s.f.	Ceramic Tile		270 s.f.
6″ Ceiling Insulation		1,440 s.f.	Vinyl Tile		60 s.f.
1″ x 24″ Slab Insulation		94 l.f.	Oak Flooring		800 s.f.
Windows (casement)		5	Carpet		38 s.y.
			Slate		56 s.f.

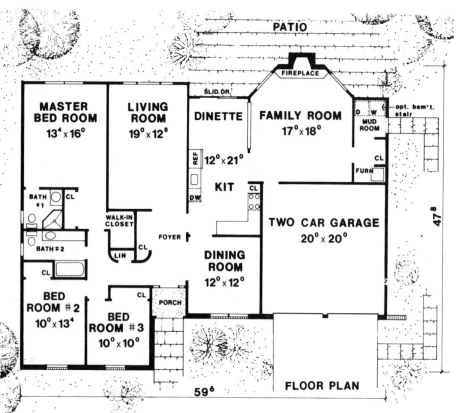

PATIO

FIREPLACE

SLID. DR.

| MASTER BED ROOM 13⁴ x 16⁰ | LIVING ROOM 19⁰ x 12⁸ | DINETTE | FAMILY ROOM 17⁰ x 18⁰ | opt. bsm't. stair |

REF 12⁰ x 21⁰

D W

MUD ROOM

BATH #1   CL

KIT   CL

CL

FURN

WALK-IN CLOSET

BATH #2

LIN   CL

FOYER

DW

CL

TWO CAR GARAGE 20⁰ x 20⁰

CL

DINING ROOM 12⁰ x 12⁰

BED ROOM #2 10⁰ x 13⁴

CL

BED ROOM #3 10⁰ x 10⁰

PORCH

47⁸

59⁶

FLOOR PLAN

THE DRYDEN

A sparkling, three bedroom ranch of pleasant proportions, with a touch of provincial flair. A roomy entrance foyer with a raised, rounded ceiling provides direct access to the front formal dining room, rear living room, bedroom wing and rear informal wing. The conveniently located kitchen includes a large breakfast area and sliding doors to the patio, as well as access to the fantastic family room. This family room features its dramatic angled "prow-shape," a soaring cathedral ceiling and a brick fireplace. There are an abundance of closets in the bedroom wing, as well as a private master suite with a separate shower and bath. The home also includes a two car garage and a mud room. Plans for an optional full basement are included in the blueprints.

MATERIAL LIST

Concrete	(s)	59 c.y.	Doors (exterior)	2
	(b)	82 c.y.	(ext. sliding)	1
Brick Veneer		306 s.f.	(interior swing)	11
Framing Lumber	(s)	7,017 b.f.	(int. closet)	5
	(b)	8,496 b.f.	Wood Shingles	1,110 s.f.
Wall Sheathing		1,416 s.f.	Asphalt Shingles	2,660 s.f.
Roof Sheathing		2,660 s.f.	½'' Gypsum Drywall	5,874 s.f.
3½'' Wall Insulation		1,510 s.f.	Ceramic Tile	176 s.f.
6'' Ceiling Insulation		1,920 s.f.	Vinyl Tile	285 s.f.
1'' x 24'' Slab Insulation		172 l.f.	Carpet	124 s.y.
Windows (single hung)		9		

AREA DATA	Living Area	1,881 s.f.
	Opt. Basement	716 s.f.

THE PLYMOUTH

AREA DATA	First Floor	941 s.f.
	Second Floor	885 s.f.
	Apartment	596 s.f.
	Basement	918 s.f.

A charming two story home with Dutch gambrel roof styling for the main body of the home, plus an appealing one story wing that disguises the fact that the home also includes a lovely one-bedroom apartment. In the main house, the entrance foyer leads to a very large L-shaped living and dining room. Adjacent to the dining area is a luxurious kitchen and adjoining breakfast nook. The second floor includes three bedrooms, plenty of closets, two spacious baths and an expansion attic. A laundry-mud room adjacent to the kitchen serves as the link to the apartment, which includes a modest living room, bedroom, eat-in kitchen and full bath. There is a private entrance to the apartment from the front portico.

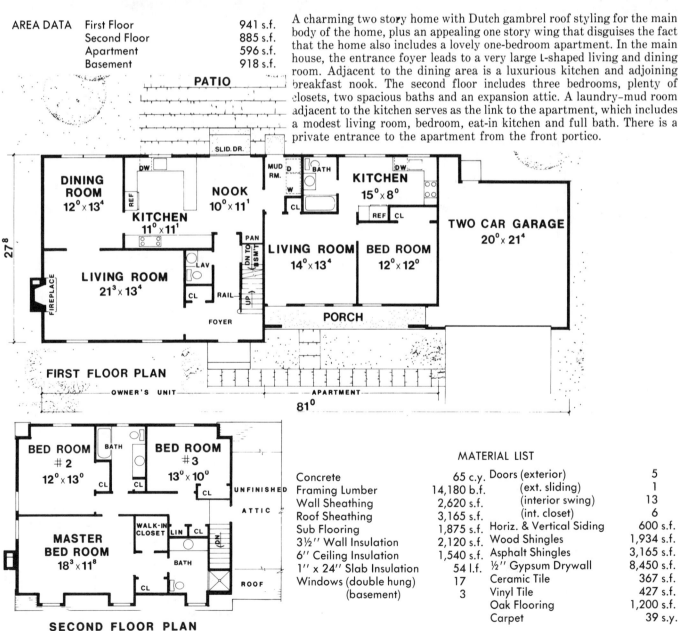

FIRST FLOOR PLAN

SECOND FLOOR PLAN

MATERIAL LIST				
Concrete	65 c.y.	Doors (exterior)		5
Framing Lumber	14,180 b.f.	(ext. sliding)		1
Wall Sheathing	2,620 s.f.	(interior swing)		13
Roof Sheathing	3,165 s.f.	(int. closet)		6
Sub Flooring	1,875 s.f.	Horiz. & Vertical Siding		600 s.f.
3½" Wall Insulation	2,120 s.f.	Wood Shingles		1,934 s.f.
6" Ceiling Insulation	1,540 s.f.	Asphalt Shingles		3,165 s.f.
1" x 24" Slab Insulation	54 l.f.	½" Gypsum Drywall		8,450 s.f.
Windows (double hung)	17	Ceramic Tile		367 s.f.
(basement)	3	Vinyl Tile		427 s.f.
		Oak Flooring		1,200 s.f.
		Carpet		39 s.y.

THE KIMBERLY

A large, distinctive looking, two story, Tudor style home, gracious in size yet designed for a site of modest frontage. The spacious entrance foyer, two stories high at one point, provides direct access to all rooms. A generous sized dining room is to the left of the foyer. A mud room–laundry area, including a pantry, closets, door to the yard and lavatory, connects the dining room and the U-shaped kitchen with its bayed breakfast area. The family room features a cathedral ceiling and sliding doors to the patio. The sunken living room includes a two-way fireplace which it shares with the family room. The second floor provides four generous sized bedrooms, two full baths and a lavish master suite.

AREA DATA	First Floor	1,369 s.f.
	Second Floor	1,321 s.f.
	Basement	959 s.f.

FIRST FLOOR PLAN

BRKFST RM 10'x11'4
KITCH 11'4 10'0
DW
MUD RM
CL
CL PANTRY
FAMILY RM 13'0x18'0 CATHEDRAL CL'G
REF
LAV
UP
DN
FOYER
SLID. DR
PATIO
LOGS
RAISED HEARTH
FIREPL
LIVING ROOM 19'0 x 15'0
DN
TWO CAR GARAGE
CL
DINING ROOM 16'0 x 11'0
PORTICO
47'4
44'8

SECOND FLOOR PLAN

STORAGE
CL
UPPER FAMILY RM
BATH
DRESSING RM
CL
CL
BED RM-4 12'8 x 11'5
BATH
W.I. CL
UPPER FOYER
DN
RAIL
BED RM-3 13'8 x 11'5
CL
BED RM-2 12'0 x 13'5
CL
LIN
MASTER BED RM 13'0 x 19'0

MATERIAL LIST

Concrete	100 c.y.	Doors (exterior)	2
Brick Veneer	427 s.f.	(ext. sliding)	1
Framing Lumber	13,225 b.f.	(interior swing)	14
Wall Sheathing	2,360 s.f.	(int. closet)	6
Roof Sheathing	2,235 s.f.	Stucco	1,850 s.f.
Sub Flooring	2,375 s.f.	Asphalt Shingles	2,235 s.f.
3½'' Wall Insulation	2,570 s.f.	½'' Gypsum Drywall	9,600 s.f.
6'' Ceiling Insulation	1,960 s.f.	Ceramic Tile	114 s.f.
1'' x 24'' Slab Insulation	54 l.f.	Vinyl Tile	430 s.f.
Windows (double hung)	22	Oak Flooring	1,732 s.f.
Windows (fixed)	1	Carpet	32 s.y.

THE SEVILLE

Distinctive Spanish styling and a contemporary floor plan distinguish this moderate sized, U-shaped ranch home. Three distinct wings wrap around an interior court that can be developed as a patio and pool. A large arcaded front portico serves as a gracious exterior entry to the home. A dramatic center hall and foyer is flanked by the living and dining rooms; both feature soaring cathedral ceilings and arcaded enclosures. From the center hall, a glass enclosed gallery leads to either the bedroom wing or kitchen. The spacious kitchen also includes a breakfast area accessible to the courtyard. The bedroom wing contains three bedrooms, including a lovely master suite that faces the courtyard.

AREA DATA

Living Area	1,650 s.f.
Opt. Basement	1,650 s.f.

MATERIAL LIST

Concrete	(s)	60 c.y.
	(b)	102 c.y.
Framing	(s)	9,704 b.f.
	(b)	13,366 b.f.
Wall Sheathing		2,050 s.f.
Roof Sheathing		2,840 s.f.
3½'' Wall Insulation		1,870 s.f.
6'' Ceiling Insulation		1,680 s.f.
1'' x 24'' Slab Insulation		224 l.f.
Windows (alum. sgl. hung)		15
(fixed glass)		9
Doors (exterior)		1
(ext. sliding)		6
(interior swing)		12
(int. closet)		4
Stucco		2,050 s.f.
Spanish Clay Tile		2,840 s.f.
½'' Gypsum Drywall		6,163 s.f.
Ceramic Tile		241 s.f.
Quarry Tile		166 s.f.
Vinyl Tile		259 s.f.
Carpet		104 s.y.

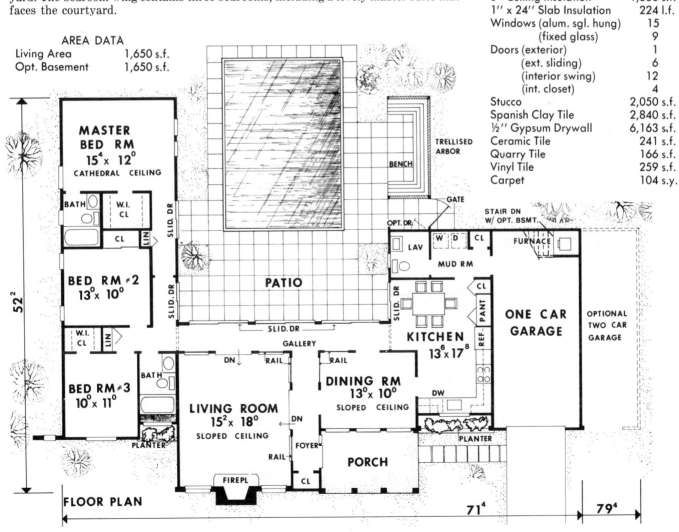

FLOOR PLAN

CONSTRUCTION BLUEPRINT INFORMATION

CONSTRUCTION BLUEPRINTS ARE AVAILABLE FOR ALL HOMES. THESE PROFESSIONALLY DRAWN, SCALED, DRAWINGS INCLUDE THE FOLLOWING INFORMATION:

1) FLOOR PLANS
   INCLUDE ALL DIMENSIONS, STRUCTURAL FRAMING, ELECTRICAL, PLUMBING, DIAGRAMS, LAYOUT INFORMATION, FLOORING MATERIALS.

2) ELEVATIONS
   INCLUDE ALL VIEWS OF HOME, WINDOWS, DOORS, ROOF OVERHANGS, SIDING MATERIALS.

3) CONSTRUCTION SECTIONS AND DETAILS
   INCLUDE DETAILED INFORMATION ON HOW TO CONSTRUCT THE HOME, FLOOR HEIGHTS, ROOF PITCHES, FRAMING MEMBERS.

4) FOUNDATION OR BASEMENT PLANS
   INCLUDE ALL DIMENSIONS TO LAYOUT FOUNDATION, CHEEKS, STEPS, FOOTINGS, ETC. MOST PLANS COME TO YOU WITH SLAB AND BASEMENT VERSIONS - YOU CAN INTERCHANGE.

5) FIREPLACE DETAILS, STAIR SECTIONS, KITCHEN INFORMATION, WINDOW AND DOOR SCHEDULES, MISCELLANEOUS DETAILS.
   INCLUDE ALL THE SPECIALIZED DATA REQUIRED BY YOU AND YOUR CONTRACTORS.

WHERE OPTIONS ARE SHOWN ON THE BROCHURES THESE WILL AUTOMATICALLY BE INCLUDED IN THE CONSTRUCTION DRAWINGS - YOU DO NOT HAVE TO SPECIFY YOUR ALTERNATES.

REVERSE PLANS (MIRROR PRINTS IN WHICH EVERYTHING IS PRINTED IN REVERSE) ARE AVAILABLE. IF YOU SPECIFY, ONE SET OF MIRROR PRINTS WILL BE SUBSTITUTED IN THE STANDARD PACKAGE OF FOUR SETS AT NO EXTRA CHARGE.

YOUR COMPLETE BLUEPRINT PACKAGE ALSO INCLUDES THE FOLLOWING:

EVERY ORDER INCLUDES ONE COPY OF A DETAILED SEVEN PAGE OUTLINE SPECIFICATION AND ONE COPY OF A MATERIALS AND LUMBER LIST.

THERE IS ALSO A DETAILED GUIDE ON HOW TO USE THE PLANS, AND HOW TO MAKE CHANGES, IF NECESSARY, PLUS HELPFUL INFORMATION ON GETTING STARTED.

FURTHERMORE, TO AID YOU IN CONSERVING ENERGY, THERE ARE EXTRA BLUEPRINTS INCLUDED, WHICH COMPLEMENT THE ENERGY-SAVING INFORMATION INCLUDED IN THIS BOOK.

Information regarding the ordering of stock plans for the homes in this book may be obtained by writing the author, Jerold L. Axelrod, Architect, 275 Broadhollow Road., Melville, N.Y. 11746